LOGOS
LATIN

LOGOS LATIN

WRITTEN BY JULIE GARFIELD
ILLUSTRATED BY MARK BEAUCHAMP

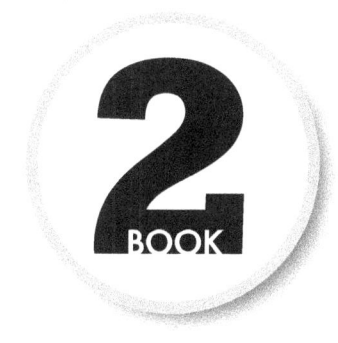

LOGOS PRESS

Moscow, Idaho

© 2010 Logos Press

Published by Logos Press
a division of Faith Ministries, Inc.
110 Baker St.
Moscow, ID 83843
www.logospressonline.com

Printed in the United States of America

ISBN-13 978-1-935000-25-9
ISBN-10 1-935000-25-9
First Edition

Cover & page design by Lisa Beyeler

All rights reserved. No part of this publication may be reproduced, stored in a retrevial system, or transmitted in any form or by any means—for example, electronic, photocopy, recording—without the prior written permission of the publisher. The only exception is brief quotations in reviews.

Table of Contents

INTRODUCTION — 13

PRONUNCIATION GUIDE & GRAMMAR ABBREVIATIONS — 15

UNIT ONE

List 1		Back to School	19
	Lesson 1	Present tense, First Conjugation	21
	Lesson 2	Five Noun Cases, First & Second Declensons	25
List 2		More Back to School	29
	Lesson 3	Second Conjugation, Future Tense	31
	Lesson 4	Accusative Case & Pattern 2 Sentences	35
List 3		At Home After School	39
	Lesson 5	Imperfect Tense; Preposition *Ad*	41
	Lesson 6	Preposition *In* & the Ablative Case	45
Unit 1 Review			49

UNIT TWO

List 4		A Visit to the Farm	53
	Lesson 7	Second Declension Neuter	55
	Lesson 8	The Use of *Possum*, The Infinitive of Verbs	59
List 5		More on the Farm	63
	Lesson 9	Verb stem	65
	Lesson 10	Singular Commands	69
List 6		Work on the Farm	73
	Lesson 11	Plural Commands, Questions	75
	Lesson 12	Preposition *Cum*	79
Unit 2 Review			83

UNIT THREE

List 7		A Visit to Rome	89
	Lesson 13	Genitive Case: Identifying Declension, Base	91
	Lesson 14	Practice with the Genitive Case	95
List 8		Birthday Party	99
	Lesson 15	More Practice with the Genitive Case	101
	Lesson 16	Dative Case and Indirect Objects	103
List 9		Illness	107
	Lesson 17	Noun Case Review	109
	Lesson 18	More Practice with Cases	111
Unit 3 Review			115

UNIT FOUR

List 10		Colors and Clothes (introduce 3rd declension)	121
	Lesson 19	Noun-Adjective Agreement: Gender	123
	Lesson 20	Noun-Adjective Agreement: Number	127
List 11		Visit to the Jewelry Store	129
	Lesson 21	Noun-Adjective Agreement: Case	131
	Lesson 22	More Practice with Adjectives	135
List 12		Trouble with the Shopkeeper	137
	Lesson 23	Review of *Possum*, Infinitives, Noun-Adj. Agreement	139
	Lesson 24	Review of Questions & Verbs	143
Unit 4 Review			147

UNIT FIVE

List 13		Ordinal Numbers	153
	Lesson 25	Cardinal Numbers & Ordinal Numbers	155
	Lesson 26	Practice with Ordinal & Cardinal Numbers	159
List 14		Exploring a Cave	163
	Lesson 27	Adverbs	165
	Lesson 28	Dative Case Review; More Practice with Adverbs	167
List 15		Adventure at the River	169
	Lesson 29	Adverb Review	171
	Lesson 30	Review of Numbers and Adverbs; Macaronic Story	175
Unit 5 Review			177

UNIT SIX

List 16		Robbers!	183
	Lesson 31	Third Declension	185
	Lesson 32	More Third Declension, Third Declension I-Stem	189
List 17		Courtroom	193
	Lesson 33	Practice with English to Latin Sentences	195
	Lesson 34	Review of Genitive and Accusative Cases	199
List 18		Government	201
	Lesson 35	Review of Declension Chants, Base Nouns & Verb Tense	203
	Lesson 36	Declension Identification, Noun-Adj. Agreement	209
Unit 6 Review			213

UNIT SEVEN

List 19		Insects and Reptiles	219
	Lesson 37	Third Declension Neuter	221
	Lesson 38	Third Declension Neuter and Accusative Case	225
List 20		Rock Quarry	229
	Lesson 39	Third Declension and the Dative Case	231
	Lesson 40	Sentence Practice with Patterns 1, 2, 3, and Declension Nouns	235
List 21		Parades & Pretending	239
	Lesson 41	Third Declension and the Genitive Case	241
	Lesson 42	Review of Genitive and Dative Cases	245
Unit 7 Review			249

UNIT EIGHT

List 22		Picnic	255
	Lesson 43	Introduction to linking verb	257
	Lesson 44	Case review, more practice with the linking verb	261
List 23		At the Seashore	263
	Lesson 45	Linking verb future tense	265
	Lesson 46	More practice with the linking verb	269
List 24		Entertainment	273
	Lesson 47	Linking verb imperfect tense	275
	Lesson 48	Question review, linking verb practice	279
Unit 8 Review			281

UNIT NINE

Lesson 49	Review Lists 1-9 and Units 1-3		285
Lesson 50	Review Lists 10-18 and Units 4-6		289
Lesson 51	Review Lists 19-24 and Units 7-8		295
Lesson 52	Translate Story		299

ACTIVITY PAGES

List 1	Matching Game	305
List 2	Drawing a Classroom	306
List 3	Word Search	307
List 4	Color a Farmyard	308
List 5	Comic Strip	309
List 6	Crossword Puzzle	310
List 7	Postcard from Rome	311
List 8	Color a Birthday Party	312
List 9	Word Search	313
List 10	Color-by-Number	314
List 11	Anagram	315
List 12	Crossword Puzzle	316
List 13	Color the Jewels	317
List 14	Word Search	318
List 15	Macaronic Story	319
List 16	Solve a Crime	320
List 17	Crossword Puzzle	321
List 18	Vocabulary Drawing	322
List 19	Matching Game	323
List 20	Word Search	324
List 21	Macaronic Fairytale	325
List 22	Anagram	326
List 23	Draw the Seashore	327
List 24	Macaronic Story	328
Review Lists 1-9	Giant Crossword Puzzle	329
Review Lists 10-18	Name What You See	330
Review Lists 19-24	Word Search	331
Story Illustration	Illustrate Billy Goats Gruff	332

REFERENCE PAGES

A Note About Chants	335
Verb Chants	336
Noun Chants	338
Pronoun Chants	340
Jingles and Nifty Sayings	341
Latin Verb Tense Chart I	342
Latin Noun Endings Chart I	343
Psalm 23	344
The Lord's Prayer	345
Visual Aid: Verb Stem Flower	346
Visual Aid: Nutshell	347

GLOSSARY

Latin to English	349
English to Latin	357

INDEX

	365

 Introduction

Welcome to LOGOS LATIN, BOOK 2. You have successfully traveled through LOGOS LATIN, BOOK 1 and now you are ready to begin a new phase in your Latin journey. Sometimes you will revisit places you encountered in BOOK 1 such as home or school, the city or the farm. But this time you will see and experience more because you know more Latin. You now have the ability to read and translate more detailed stories about these places. You will be able to accompany Iulius, his sister Iulia, and their friend Saxum on their adventures. You will meet their friends Claudius and Claudia.

Your journey will also take you into new Latin territory, as well as re-traveling through Latin vocabulary and grammar you already know. You will meet a new noun family, the *third declension*. You will learn uses for the genitive and dative cases of nouns. You will learn how to make questions and give commands, and how to describe nouns with adjectives, and much more. Each time you learn a new piece of Latin information, you can travel a little farther down the road, and the journey becomes more interesting.

Enjoy rest stops along the way. The "Tidbits" sections contain information about Roman life and culture. "Derivative Digging" explores English words that come from Latin. Most vacation trips include places visited just for fun. Check out the Activities section in the back of the book for some enjoyable side trips.

The road becomes steeper and more difficult in LOGOS LATIN 2 but that is part of the challenge. Think of yourself as a mountain climber who is out to conquer a higher peak than the one you climbed last year. You will need to train diligently for this climb by regular study, attentiveness, and by asking good questions. It may be hard at times but when you reach the top and see how far you have come it will be worth it!

I look forward to being your guide on this next stretch of your Latin journey. Have a good trip!

Vale,

Julie Garfield

Pronunciation Guide and Grammar Abbreviations

Logos Latin uses the Classical pronunciation of Latin. (In the Logos Latin 2 DVD, however, the letter *v* is pronounced as a "v" not a "w," following Ecclesiastical Latin.)

VOWELS

In Latin, vowels only have two pronunciations: long and short. In conversation, long vowels are held twice as long as short vowels. Long vowels are marked with a *macron*, a line over the vowel (e.g., ō). Vowels without a macron are short vowels.

When spelling a word, including the macron is important in order to determine the meaning of the word.

Long Vowels

ā	like *a* in *water*:	māter
ē	like *eigh* in *weigh*:	pēs
ī	like *i* in *chlorine*:	vīvo
ō	like *o* in *hole*:	creō
ū	like *oo* in *food*:	mūtō

Short Vowels

a	like *a* in *fall*:	caput
e	like *e* in *red*:	semper
i	like *i* in *lick*:	nihil
o	like *o* in *Roman*:	domus
u	like *u* in *pull*:	oculus

DIPHTHONGS

Two vowel sounds collapsed together into one syllable are called *dipthongs*. The Latin dipthongs are:

ae	like *y* in *style*:	copiae
au	like *ou* in *mouse*:	audeō
ei	like *ai* in *slain*:	deinde
eu	like *eew* in *Tuesday*:	Orpheus
oe	like *oi* in *spoil*:	moenia
ui	like *ew* in *stew*:	huius

CONSONANTS

Latin consonants are pronounced the same as English consonants with the following exceptions:

c	like *c* in *call*	never soft like *city*, *cell*, or *space*
g	like *g* in *golf*	never soft like *Germany*, *geography*, or *germ*
v	like *w* in *wow*	never like *vermin*, *victory*, or *varnish*
s	like *s* in *sister*	never like *easy*, *wise*, or *please*
ch	like *ch* in *chorus*	never like *chain*, *child*, or *chicken*
r	is trilled	like a cat purring
i	like *y* in *yes*	when used before a vowel at the beginning of a word or between two vowels within a word; at most other times it's used as a vowel

GRAMMAR ABBREVIATIONS
(as taught in Shurley English)

SN	Subject Noun
DO	Direct Object
IO	Indirect Object
PNA	Possessive Noun Adjective
OP	Object of Preposition
PrN	Predicate Noun
Adj	Adjective
V	Verb
V-t	Verb transitive
LV	Linking Verb
INF	Infinitive
Imp	Imperative (command)
Adv	Adverb
P	Preposition
C	Conjunction
C (in front of other abbreviations) (ie: CSN = compound subject noun)	Compound

SENTENCE PATTERNS

The pattern of a sentence is the order of its main parts. The patterns taught at this level are:

SN V (P1)　　　　　　　　　　subject noun, verb - pattern 1

SN V-t DO (P2)　　　　　　　subject noun, verb-transitive, direct object - pattern 2

SN V-t IO DO (P3)　　　　　subject noun, verb-transitive, indirect object - pattern 3

SN LV PrN (P4)　　　　　　　subject noun, linking verb, predicate noun - pattern 4

1 List One: Back to School

VOCABULARY

Memorize the following Latin words and their translations.

Word	Derivative	Translation
1. discipulus	_____	*boy student*
2. discipula	_____	*girl student*
3. magister	_____	*male teacher*
4. magistra	_____	*female teacher*
5. historia	_____	*history*
6. arithmētica	_____	*arithmetic*
7. littera *	_____	*letter of the alphabet*

Litterae, the plural of *littera,* can mean "literature."

8. liber	_____	*book*
9. recitō	_____	*recite, read aloud*
10. rogō	_____	*ask*

A *derivative* is an English word which comes from Latin. But there are two qualifications it must have:

    1. similar spelling
    2. similar meaning

REVIEW WORDS

Review lists throughout the book may include words from Logos Latin 1. The definitions are included in the glossary at the end of the book.

1. Quid est? — *What is it?*
2. Quis est? — *Who is it?*
3. salvē — *hello*
4. valē — *good bye*
5. notā bene — *note well* (abbreviated as N.B.)
6. et — *and*

REVIEW CHANTS

PRESENT TENSE VERB ENDING

-ō	-mus
-s	-tis
-t	-nt

FIRST DECLENSION

-a	-ae
-ae	-ārum
-ae	-īs
-am	-ās
-ā	-īs

SECOND DECLENSION

-us	-ī
-ī	-ōrum
-ō	-īs
-um	-ōs
-ō	-īs

1 Lesson One: Back to School

A. PRESENT TENSE VERBS

In Latin, verb endings are extremely important because they tell us who is doing the action of the verb and when the action is happening. In the present tense, the action of the verb is happening now. Review the present tense verb endings and their meanings in the chart below:

PRESENT TENSE VERB ENDINGS (CHANT)

Person	Singular	Plural
1st	-ō - *I*	-mus - *we*
2nd	-s - *you*	-tis - *you all*
3rd	-t - *he, she, it*	-nt - *they*

The first person always includes "I" — either "I" *by myself* (singular) or "I" *with someone else*, which makes "we" (plural):

> **I** am a new student. (singular)
> **We** are new students. (plural)

The second person is used when you are talking directly to someone:

> **You** are my friend. (singular)
> **You all** are my friends. (plural)

The third person is used when you are talking about someone else:

> **He** is the teacher. (singular)
> **They** are the teachers. (plural)

Est Magister

B. FIRST CONJUGATION VERBS - "A" Family

Translate forms of *rogō* and *recitō* in the present tense. Both of these verbs are from the first conjugation, or the "A" Family of verbs because the vowel *A* appears before all of the verb endings except the first person singular *ō*. <u>Underline</u> the Latin verb endings before you translate. Highlight each *a* which appears before the verb endings.

1. rogāmus _____
2. recitat _____
3. rogō _____
4. recitātis _____
5. rogās _____
6. recitant _____

First Conjugation: The "A" Verb Family

C. PRESENT TENSE HELPING VERBS: am, is, are, do, does

There are three ways to translate present tense verbs:

1. No helping verb — *We ask*
2. Choose from *am, is, are* — *We are asking*
3. Choose from *do, does* — *We do ask*

Translate the present tense verbs below in three ways. The first one is done as an example.

1. recitās — <u>You recite, you are reciting, or you do recite</u>
2. rogat _____
3. recitāmus _____
4. rogātis _____

Lesson One

5. recitō _____

6. rogant _____

D. DERIVATIVE DIGGING

Look up the word *magistrate* in an English dictionary and write its meaning on the lines provided.

magistrate - _____

_____

What is its Latin origin (What Latin word does it come from)? _____

est Iūlius

est Iūlia

Lesson One

Lesson Two: Back to School

A. NOUNS & THE NOMINATIVE CASE

Latin nouns are also organized into families of endings. These are called *declensions*. Let's review some declensions we have learned before (these are also chants).

FIRST DECLENSION ("A" Family Nouns)

Case	Singular	Plural
Nominative	-a	-ae
Genitive	-ae	-ārum
Dative	-ae	-īs
Accusative	-am	-ās
Ablative	-ā	-īs

SECOND DECLENSION ("US" Family Nouns)

Case	Singular	Plural
Nominative	-us	-ī
Genitive	-ī	-ōrum
Dative	-ō	-īs
Accusative	-um	-ōs
Ablative	-ō	-īs

These noun endings tell you what part of speech a noun is, and whether it is singular or plural. Noun endings are called *case endings*.

Each case in Latin relates to a part of speech in English. The **nominative case** is used for subject nouns. In this lesson we only deal with the nominative case, but you need to know the names of all five noun cases.

The noun cases are spelled below, along with a way to remember them:

Nominative	*No*
Genitive	*Gentle*
Dative	*Dad*
Accusative	*Accuses*
Ablative	*Apples*

B. MAKING NOUNS PLURAL

To make a noun plural in the nominative case, remove the nominative singular ending and then add the plural ending.

	Nominative Singular	Nominative Plural
First Declension	-a	-ae
Second Declension	-us	-ī

Now study the examples below.

NOMINATIVE SINGULAR

discipula *girl student*
discipulus *boy student*

NOMINATIVE PLURAL

discipulae *girl students*
discipulī *boy students*

Lesson Two

C. TRANSLATION – PATTERN 1 SENTENCES

The pattern of a sentence is the order of its main parts. Pattern 1 sentences simply contain a subject noun and a verb (SN V P1). The following are Pattern 1 sentences. Translate each one. <u>Underline</u> endings on both the noun and the verb and label parts of speech above each word. This should be done before you translate. Use SN as the label for subject nouns and V as the label for verbs.

N.B. (Notā Bene) *A singular verb requires a singular subject noun. A plural verb requires a plural subject noun.

*Often in books, *nota bene* is abbreviated N.B. When you see N.B. or *nota bene*, you should pay special attention to what is written afterward — it is important!

1. Discipula rogat. _____

2. Magister* recitat. _____

3. Magistrī recitant. _____

4. Discipulae rogant. _____

*Some nouns in the second declension ("Us" Family) end in **-er** in the nominative singular.

D. TIDBIT

Did you know that the ancient Roman alphabet had only twenty-three letters? Modern English uses the Roman alphabet but three letters have been added. Can you guess which three?

_____

_____

_____

2 List Two: More Back to School

VOCABULARY
Memorize the following Latin words and their translations:

Word	Derivative	Translation
1. lūdus	_____	*school, game*
2. amīcus	_____	*male friend*
3. amīca	_____	*female friend*
4. mensa	_____	*desk, table*
5. sella	_____	*seat, chair*
6. tabula	_____	*map, board, tablet*
7. numerus	_____	*number*
8. geōgraphia	_____	*geography*
9. fābula	_____	*story*
10. studēo	_____	*study*
11. monstrō	_____	*show, point out*
12. numerō	_____	*count*
13. rēspondeō	_____	*answer*
14. habeō	_____	*have, hold*
15. spectō	_____	*look at*

List Two

REVIEW WORDS

1. hodiē* — *today*
2. crās* — *tomorrow*
3. schola — *class, classroom*
4. stylus — *pencil*
5. charta — *piece of paper*
6. recitō — *recite, read aloud*
7. rogō — *ask*

*Both *hodiē* and *crās* are vocabulary words from Logos Latin 1. However, they are also vocabulary words for this year, appearing later, in List 14.

REVIEW CHANT

FUTURE TENSE VERB ENDING

-bō	-bimus
-bis	-bitis
-bit	-bunt

Quid est?
Est _____

List Two

3 Lesson Three: More Back to School

A. SECOND CONJUGATION VERBS — "E" Family

We already know that the family resemblance for first conjugation verbs is the vowel *a* which appears before the verb endings (except first person singular). In the second conjugation, the vowel *e* appears before all verb endings.

First Conjugation: "A" Family

rogō	rogāmus
rogās	rogātis
rogāt	rogant

Second Conjugation: "E" Family

studeō	studēmus
studēs	studētis
studet	student

List the three second conjugation or "E" Family verbs from List 2:

_____

_____

_____

B. FUTURE TENSE VERBS

We use the future tense to talk about something that will happen but which has not happened yet. The helping verb for this tense is *will*.

FUTURE TENSE VERB ENDINGS (CHANT)

Person	Singular	Plural
1st	-bō - *I will*	-bimus - *we will*
2nd	-bis - *you will*	-bitis - *you all will*
3rd	-bit - *he, she, it will*	-bunt - *they will*

You should recognize the *present tense* endings contained within this chant. Highlight those present tense endings on the chart.

C. TRANSLATION

HODIĒ (*today*)
Translate these sentences using the present tense to show what is happening now. Label subject nouns and verbs and underline their endings. *Hodiē* is an adverb(Adv).

    SN   V
1. Studē<u>mus</u> hodie.   We study today.

2. Hodiē Iūlia numerat. _____

3. Hodiē amīcī recitant. _____

4. Respondētis hodiē. _____

5. Hodiē spectās. _____

Translate these sentences into Latin:

6. I count. _____

7. I am counting. _____

8. I do count. _____

CRĀS (*tomorrow*)
Translate these sentences using the future tense to show what will happen.
Label and underline. *Crās* is an adverb (Adv). *Et* is a *conjunction* (C). When subject nouns are linked by *et* they are *compound subject nouns*. Label them CSN.

   Adv CSN C CSN   V
1. Crās Iūlius et Iūlia monstrābunt. Julius and Julia will show tomorrow.

2. Amīca numerābit crās. _____

3. Crās respondēbimus. _____

4. Studēbō crās. _____

5. Crās spectābitis. _____

Translate this sentence into Latin:

6. You will have. _____

D. HELPING VERBS

Review the helping verbs for the present tense by filling in those that are missing:

1. am _____

2. _____

3. _____

4. do _____

5. _____

Iulius monstrat

What is the helping verb for the future tense? _____

Lesson Three   33

E. DERIVATIVE DIGGING

The English word *enumerate* is another derivative for *numerō*. Enumerate can simply mean to count something, but it also has another meaning. Look up that meaning in an English dictionary and write it on the lines below:

_____

_____

_____

Lesson Three

 # Lesson Four: More Back to School

A. NOUN CASES

Using the jingle we have learned in Lesson 2, write out the five noun cases from memory.

Five Noun Cases

NO _____

GENTLE _____

DAD _____

ACCUSES _____

APPLES _____

What case is used for subject nouns? _____

Consider the example below:

    SN   V   SN   V
Discipula recitat.   *The girl student reads aloud.*

ACCUSATIVE CASE AND PATTERN 2 SENTENCES

The Pattern 1 sentence above tells us what the girl student is doing, but it does not tell us what she is reading aloud. To answer that question, we need a *direct object*.

Lesson Four

In Latin, direct objects go in the **accusative case**. We call this type of sentence *Pattern 2*. A Pattern 2 sentence contains: a subject noun (SN), a verb (called a verb transitive, or V-t, when there is a DO), and a direct object. Study the Pattern 2 sentence below.

    SN DO V-t   SN V-t DO
   Discipul<u>a</u> fabul<u>am</u> recit<u>at</u>.   *The girl student reads aloud a story.*

In English, we depend on word order to tell us what part of speech a noun is. In Latin, the endings tell us whether a noun is a subject or a direct object.

The example above used first declension nouns. Let's do another sentence containing second declension nouns.

    SN DO V-t   SN V-t DO
   Discipul<u>us</u> numer<u>um</u> stud<u>et</u>.   *The boy student studies the number.*

For practice, look at these plural examples of Pattern 2 sentences:

    SN DO V-t   SN V-t DO
   Discipul<u>ae</u> fabul<u>ās</u> recita<u>nt</u>.   *The girl students read aloud the stories.*

    SN DO V-t   SN V-t DO
   Discipul<u>ī</u> numer<u>ōs</u> stude<u>nt</u>.   *The boy students study the numbers.*

N.B. The direct object is often placed *in front of* the verb in Latin.

B. ACCUSATIVE ENDINGS

Put accusative endings on the following first and second declension nouns.

Noun	Accusative Singular	Accusative Plural
1. lūdus	_____	_____
2. mensa	_____	_____
3. amīca	_____	_____

Lesson Four

C. TRANSLATION

Translate these Pattern 2 sentences into English. <u>Underline</u> word endings and label parts of speech before translating.

1. Iūlius et amīcus geōgraphiam student. _____

_____

2. Magistra tabulam monstrat. _____

3. Iūlia geōgraphiam nōn studet. _____

4. Iūlia librum spectat. _____

5. Iūlia litterās numerat. _____

6. Magistra Iūliam spectat. _____

7. Iūlia geōgraphiam studēbit! _____

Quid est?

Est _____

D. TIDBIT

A number of Latin words come from Greek. One such word is *geōgraphia*. The word *geo-* means earth, and *-graphia* comes from the Greek *graphein*, meaning to write.

3 List Three: At Home After School

VOCABULARY

Memorize the following Latin words and their translations:

Word	Derivative	Translation
1. māter		*mother*
2. pater		*father*
3. soror		*sister*
4. frāter		*brother*
5. servus		*slave, servant*
6. ancilla		*maidservant*
7. focus		*hearth, fireplace*
8. cēna		*dinner, meal*
9. parō		*prepare*
10. apportō		*bring*
11. ambulō		*walk*
12. invītō		*invite*
13. vīsitō		*visit*
14. ad		*to, toward* (with acc. case)
15. in		*into* (with acc. case) or *in, on* (with abl. case)

REVIEW WORDS

1. est — *is*
2. sedeō — *sit*
3. sella — *seat, chair*
4. mensa — *table, desk*
5. amīcus — *male friend*
6. amīca — *female friend*
7. habeō — *have, hold*

REVIEW CHANT

IMPERFECT TENSE VERB ENDINGS

-bam	-bāmus
-bās	-bātis
-bat	-bant

Quid est?
Est _____

List Three

Lesson Five: At Home After School

A. IMPERFECT TENSE VERBS ENDINGS

The imperfect tense is one of two past tenses in Latin. Study the imperfect tense endings below. Highlight the present tense endings contained within these endings. The helping verbs for this tense are *was/were* or *used to*.

IMPERFECT TENSE VERB ENDINGS (CHANT)

Person	Singular	Plural
1st	-bam - *I was* (used to)	-bāmus - *we were* (used to)
2nd	-bās - *you were* (used to)	-bātis - *you all were* (used to)
3rd	-bat - *he, she, it was* (used to)	-bant - *they were* (used to)

Translate these verbs with imperfect tense endings. <u>Underline</u> endings.

1. visitābāmus _____

2. ambulābat _____

3. invitābās _____

4. parābant _____

5. apportābātis _____

6. spectabam _____

Servus cēnam parābat.

Lesson Five 41

B. PRACTICE

Translate these verbs from the present, future, and imperfect tenses into English. Underline endings. You may use your chant charts.

1. visitābunt   _____

2. ambulābātis   _____

3. invītat   _____

4. parō   _____

5. apportābās   _____

6. spectābimus   _____

C. THE PREPOSITION "AD" & THE ACCUSATIVE CASE

You probably already know that a *preposition* is a special group of words that connect a noun or a pronoun to the rest of the sentence. An *object of the preposition* is the noun or pronoun that comes after the preposition.

In Latin, the preposition *ad* is followed by an object of preposition (OP) in the accusative case. Look at the sample sentences below containing prepositional phrases:

```
SN      V       P    OP
Soror  ambulat  ad   focum.              The sister walks toward the fireplace.

SN     DO      V-t       P    OP
Frāter sellam  apportābat ad  mensam.    The brother was bringing the chair to the table.
```

D. TRANSLATION

Translate these sentences. Underline endings on the nouns and verbs. Label parts of speech. The labels you may need to use are: SN, V-t, DO, P, OP. Do not label sentence #3. We have not learned this pattern yet.

1. Iūlius amīcum invītābat.   _____

2. Amīcus Iūlium vīsitat. _____

3. Amīcus est Claudius. _____

4. Servus cēnam parābat. _____

_____

5. Ancillae cēnam apportābant ad mensam. _____

_____

6. Iūlius et Claudius ambulant ad mensam. _____

_____

7. Iūlius et Claudius cēnam habent. _____

_____

E. DERIVATIVE DIGGING

The Latin preposition *ad* is attached to many English words as a prefix. *Admit* and *addition* are two examples. Can you think of any others? Write them on the line.

_____

Mater et pater.

Lesson Five 43

6 Lesson Six: At Home After School

A. THE PREPOSITION "IN" & THE ABLATIVE CASE

This preposition takes its object of preposition in the **ablative case**, and it means *in* or *on*. Look at the examples below:

SN	V	P	OP (abl. case)		SN	V	P	OP
Frater	ambulat	in	ludō.		*The brother*	*walks*	*in*	*the school.*

SN	V	P	OP		SN	V	P	OP
Soror	ambulat	in	mensā.		*The sister*	*walks*	*on*	*the table.*

Circle or highlight the ablative singular and plural endings in the noun chants below.

FIRST DECLENSION NOUN ENDINGS (CHANT)

Case	Singular	Plural
Nom.	-a	-ae
Gen.	-ae	-ārum
Dat.	-ae	-īs
Acc.	-am	-ās
Abl.	-ā	-īs

SECOND DECLENSION NOUN ENDINGS (CHANT)

Case	Singular	Plural
Nom.	-us	-ī
Gen.	-ī	-ōrum
Dat.	-ō	-īs
Acc.	-um	-ōs
Abl.	-ō	-īs

Lesson Six 45

Study the plural examples of objects of preposition below:

in the chairs - in sellīs (ablative)

in the fireplaces - in focīs (ablative)

B. TRANSLATION

Translate the sentences below. <u>Underline</u> endings and label parts of speech. All contain prepositional phrases. You do not have to label sentence three.

1. Iūlia ambulābat ad lūdum. _____

2. Visitābit amīcam in scholā.* _____

3. Amīca est Claudia. _____

4. Iūlia et Claudia sedent in sellīs. _____

5. Magister apportat librōs ad scholam. _____

6. Discipulae studēbunt arithmēticam et historiam. _____

*Challenge Question: What is the subject in sentence #2? _____

C. VERB PRACTICE

Translate these sentences. You will need to decide whether the Latin verb is in the present, future, or imperfect tense.

1. visitābam _____

2. ambulābit _____

3. parābunt _____

4. vīsitātis _____

Translate these into Latin. Pay attention to the helping verbs.

1. We bring. _____

2. We do bring. _____

3. We are bringing. _____

D. TIDBIT

Roman boys were accompanied to and from school by a slave called a *paedagōgus*. Sometimes this slave also instructed children in manners. Greek slaves were later used in order to help Roman children learn Greek.

Unit One Review

A. VOCABULARY

From memory, translate as many of these vocabulary words as you can. Then look up any you don't remember.

1. discipulus _____

2. magistra _____

3. liber _____

4. historia _____

5. amīca _____

6. tabula _____

7. numerus _____

8. mensa _____

9. fābula _____

10. lūdus _____

11. focus _____

12. ancilla _____

13. frater _____

14. ad _____

15. cēna _____

16. pāter _____

17. servus _____

18. sella _____

19. geōgraphia _____

20. in (with abl.) _____

B. REVIEW CHANTS

Fill in these verb chants and their meanings:

PRESENT TENSE

-ō - *I*	

What are the five helping verbs for the present tense?

1._____ 2._____ 3._____ 4._____ 5._____

IMPERFECT TENSE

-bam - *I was (used to)*	

List imperfect tense helping verbs: 1._____ 2._____ 3._____

FUTURE TENSE

-bō - *I will*	

Helping verb? _____

Unit 1 Review

C. VERB PRACTICE

Translate these verbs. Underline endings.

1. recitābās _____

2. rogābunt _____

3. studēmus _____

4. monstrābam _____

5. respondēbitis _____

D. TRANSLATION

Translate the following sentences. Underline endings on nouns and verbs. Label parts of speech. Possible labels include: SN, CSN, DO, CDO, P, OP, C, V, V-t.

1. Discipulae librōs apportant ad mensam. _____

2. Magistra litteram monstrābat in tabulā. _____

3. Magistra rogat, "Quid est?" _____

3. Iūlius respondet, "Est littera!" _____

4. Iūlia ambulābit ad tabulam. _____

5. Discipulī arithmēticam parābunt. _____

E. DERIVATIVES

Give an English derivative for each of the following Latin words:

1. discipulus _____

2. liber _____

3. spectō _____

4. pater _____

5. ad _____

4 List Four: A Visit to the Farm

VOCABULARY

Memorize the following Latin words and their translations.

N.B. After the nouns, the genitive singular ending is given; after verbs, the *second principle part* (also called the *infinitive*) is given. Memorize these as well.

Word	Derivative	Translation
1. praedium, -ī		*farm*
2. horreum, -ī		*barn*
3. vacca, -ae		*cow*
4. capra, -ae		*female goat*
5. gallus, -ī		*rooster*
6. saxum, -ī		*rock*
7. mannulus, -ī		*pony*
8. faenum, -ī		*hay*
9. prātum, -ī		*meadow*
10. pōmum, -ī		*fruit*
11. dō, -āre		*give*
12. secō, -āre		*cut*
13. struō, -āre		*pile up*
14. canō, -āre		*crow*
15. possum, posse		*be able*

List Four

REVIEW WORDS

1. avus, -ī — *grandfather*
2. avia, -ae — *grandmother*
3. agricola, -ae — *farmer*
4. dominus, -ī — *lord, master*
5. gallīna, -ae — *hen*
6. mālum, -ī — *apple*
7. stabulum, -ī — *stall, stable*
8. ovum, -ī — *egg*
9. visitō, -āre — *visit*
10. libō, -āre — *taste, sip*
11. equitō, -āre — *ride (on horseback)*
12. in (w/abl.) — *in, on*
13. liberī, ōrum — *children*
14. nōn — *not*

Quid est?

Est _____

REVIEW CHANTS (FROM LOGOS LATIN 1)

SUM CHANT - LINKING VERB (PRESENT TENSE)

sum	sumus
es	estis
est	sunt

POSSUM CHANT

possum	possumus
potes	potestis
potest	possunt

SECOND DECLENSION NEUTER

-um	-a
-ī	-ōrum
-ō	-īs
-um	-a
-ō	-īs

List Four

7 Lesson Seven: A Visit to the Farm

A. SECOND DECLENSION NEUTER

Study the second neuter noun endings below. What do you notice about the nominative and accusative endings?

SECOND DECLENSION NEUTER (CHANT)

Case	Singular	Plural
Nom.	-um	-a
Gen.	-ī	-ōrum
Dat.	-ō	-īs
Acc.	-um	-a
Abl.	-ō	-īs

Quid est?

Est _____

You should have noticed that the nominative and accusative endings look the same in second neuter. This can be tricky when translating a Pattern 2 sentence containing both a subject noun and a direct object. How do you know when a second declension neuter noun is a subject and when it is a direct object? Usually, it is best to translate the sentence in a way that makes sense. Consider the examples below:

    SN   DO   V-t
    Horreum faenum habet.   Translation #1 - *The barn has hay.*

    DO   SN   V-t
    Horreum faenum habet.   Translation #2 - *The hay has a barn.*

In this example, it makes more sense to make *horreum* the subject noun, as in translation #1.

Lesson Seven 55

Compare second declension *neuter* with its cousin, second declension. Highlight or underline the places where it is different from the neuter chant above.

SECOND DECLENSION

Case	Singular	Plural
Nom.	-us	-ī
Gen.	-ī	-ōrum
Dat.	-ō	-īs
Acc.	-um	-ōs
Abl.	-ō	-īs

N.B. The nominative and accusative *plural* endings for second declension neuter are both *-a*. Don't confuse these with endings from the first declension. Compare second declension neuter endings with the first declension:

FIRST DECLENSION

-a	-ae
-ae	-ārum
-ae	-īs
-am	-ās
-ā	-īs

Quid est?

Est _____

B. PRACTICE

Decline (put endings on) the second declension neuter noun *saxum*.

Case	Singular	Plural
Nom.	saxum	
Gen.		
Dat.		
Acc.		
Abl.		

Lesson Seven

C. THE ADVERB "NŌN"

The adverb *nōn* (not) is used to make a sentence negative. Two things to remember: 1) *Nōn* is placed in front of the verb, and 2) Whenever translating a negative sentence into English you must use the correct helping verb. Study the examples below.

Present Tense: Iūlius mannulum nōn equitat.   *Julius **is** not riding the pony.*
                                                                    or
                                                                    *Julius **does** not ride the pony.*

Future Tense: Iūlius mannulum nōn equitābit.   *Julius **will** not ride the pony.*

Imperfect Tense: Iūlius mannulum nōn equitābat.   *Julius **was** not riding the pony.*

D. TRANSLATION

Translate these sentences. <u>Underline</u> endings on nouns and verbs and label parts of speech. Some nouns are from second declension neuter, the "Um" Family.

1. Iūlius, Iūlia, et Saxum praedium visitant. _____

2. Avus et Iūlius faenum secant in prātō. _____

3. Iūlia et Saxum mannulōs equitant. _____

4. Līberī faenum struant in horreō. _____

5. Vacca faenum lībat. _____

Lesson Seven

6. Iūlius et Iūlia pōma lībant. _____

_____

7. Saxum pōmum nōn lībat. _____

E. DERIVATIVE DIGGING

Capricorn is the name of a star constellation. Try to guess what Latin word *Capricorn* comes from and then tell what animal this constellation resembles.

Capricorn comes from the Latin word _____ .

Capricorn resembles a _____ .

8 Lesson Eight: A Visit to the Farm

A. POSSUM CHANT

The verb *possum* is conjugated below. Can you find another chant which you have already learned that forms part of the Possum Chant?

possum - *I am able*	possumus - *we are able*
potes - *you are able*	potestis - *you all are able*
potest - *he, she, it is able*	possunt - *they are able*

You will recognize a pattern in the meanings. The verb *sum* means "I am." As you look at the verb *possum* you see that "I am" is part of the meaning. Now highlight the parts of the meanings which translate *sum, es, est, sumus, estis, sunt*.

You probably noticed the Sum Chant.

SUM CHANT — LINKING VERB (PRESENT TENSE)

sum - *I am*	sumus - *we are*
es - *you are*	estis - *you all are*
est - *he, she, it is*	sunt - *they are*

Quid est?

Est _____

Lesson Eight

Make sure that you can spell the *Possum* Chant correctly and give meanings. Practice by filling in the box below:

POSSUM CHANT

possum -	

B. THE INFINITIVE — THE SECOND PRINCIPAL PART

Most Latin verbs have what are called the *four principal parts*. These are listed in Latin dictionaries. On our word lists, we are currently learning only the first *two* principal parts. It is important to memorize correct spelling of both parts. The *second principal part* is called the *infinitive*. Study the examples below. What is the ending on the second principal part of these verbs? Highlight the infinitive endings.

First Principal Part	Second Principal Part (infinitive)
dō	dāre
secō	secāre
struō	struāre
canō	canāre

You should have highlighted the **-re** ending on each infinitive. The **-re** ending means *to*.

Look at the example below:

Second Principal Part (Infinitive)	Meaning of Infinitive
dāre	*to give*

Translate the other infinitives from List 4:

1. secāre _____

2. struāre _____

3. canāre _____

N.B. The verb *possum* has an irregular infinitive, *posse*.

C. INFINITIVE WITH *POSSUM*

The infinitive can be used with the verb *possum* to form a complete thought. Look at the examples below and then label and translate the rest of the sentences below. The infinitive is labeled INF.

    V   INF
    Possum equitāre.   *I am able to ride (on horseback).*

    SN   V   INF   DO
    Avus potest secāre faenum.   *Grandfather is able to cut hay.*

1. Gallus potest canāre. _____

2. Mannulī possunt lībāre faenum. _____

3. Possumus equitāre. _____

4. Iūlius et Iūlia possunt vīsitāre avum et aviam. _____

Challenge: Choose an infinitive to complete this sentence and translate.

    Possum _____

    Translation: _____

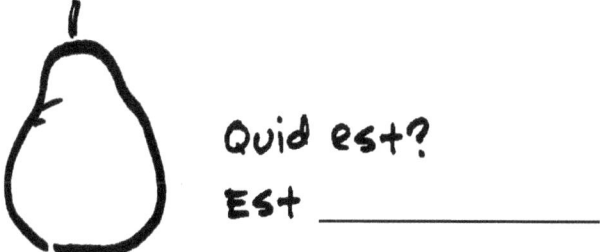

Lesson Eight

5 List Five: More on the Farm

VOCABULARY

Memorize the following Latin words and their translations. Also memorize the genitive endings of nouns and the infinitives (second principal parts) of verbs.

Word	Derivative	Translation
1. porcus, -ī		*male pig*
2. porca, -ae		*female pig*
3. porcellus, -ī		*little pig*
4. ovis, ovis*		*sheep*
5. agnus, -ī		*lamb*
6. lāna, -ae		*wool*
7. ager, agrī		*field*
8. aqua, -ae		*water*
9. tondeō, -ēre		*shear, shave, clip*
10. mulgeō, -ēre		*milk*
11. arō, -āre		*plow*
12. iuvō, -āre		*help*
13. pōtō, -āre		*drink*
14. cūrō, -āre		*care for*
15. labōrō, -āre		*work*

ovis is in the third declension which you will learn in Unit 6. It is included here along with all the other farm animals.

List Five

REVIEW LIST

1. capra, -ae — *goat*
2. vacca, -ae — *cow*
3. praedium, -ī — *farm*
4. pastor, pastōris — *shepherd*
5. dō, dāre — *give*
6. secō, secāre — *cut*
7. possum, posse — *be able*
8. struō, struāre — *pile up*
9. canō, canāre — *crow*
10. villa, -ae — *farmhouse*
11. avus, -ī — grandfather

9 Lesson Nine: More on the Farm

A. PRESENT VERB STEM

The verb stem is the basic part of the verb to which we can add endings. The present verb stem is found by removing the **-re** ending from the infinitive or second principal part of the verb. Remember **-re** means *to*. Look at these examples:

Infinitive	Verb Stem
secāre	seca-
dāre	da-

Notice that the verb stems of first conjugation verbs end in the vowel *a*. Now let's take these verb stems and add endings from the present, imperfect, and future tenses.

seca + -nt = secant (*they cut*)
seca + -bunt = secābunt (*they will cut*)
seca + -bant = secābant (*they were cutting*)

da + -mus = dāmus (*we give*)
da + -bimus = dābimus (*we will give*)
da + -bamus = dābāmus (*we were giving*)

N.B. The first person singular in the present tense does <u>not</u> contain the entire present stem. Notice that *do* and *seco* do not have an a before the ending. This is only true of first conjugation verbs ("A" Family verbs).

Verb Stem Key

☐ Past Tense
▨ Future Tense
▮ Imperfect Tense

Lesson Nine 65

Here are some second conjugation ("E" Family) verbs. Remove the **-re** from the infinitive to find the present verb stem, just as in first conjugation ("A" Family) verbs.

Infinitive	Verb Stem
tondēre	tonde-
mulgēre	mulge-

With what vowel do second conjugation verb stems end? _____

Study the second conjugation examples of verb stems with endings added.

tonde + -o = tondeō (*I shear*)
tonde + -bo = tondēbō (*I will shear*)
tonde + -bam = tondēbām (*I was shearing*)

mulge + -t = mulget (*she milks*)
mulge + -bit = mulgēbit (*she will milk*)
mulge + -bat = mulgēbat (*she was milking*)

B. PRACTICE

Underline the **present stems** of these verbs. The first one is done as an example. Tell whether or not the verb is first conjugation or second conjugation.

Verb Stems	Conjugation
1. <u>secā</u>re	1st
2. canāre	_____
3. struāre	_____
4. mulgēre	_____
5. potāre	_____
6. tondēre	_____

Lesson Nine

C. TRANSLATION

Label and translate these sentences which contain forms of the verb *possum* and infinitives. <u>Underline</u> endings on nouns and verbs, including the **-re** on the infinitives. Remember, **-re** means *to*.

1. Iūlia potest mulgēre vaccam. _____

2. Avus et Iūlius possunt arāre agrum. _____

3. Porca potest curāre porcellōs. _____

4. Potes tondēre agnum. _____

5. Possumus laborāre in villā. _____

D. DERIVATIVE DIGGING

Look up the English word *collaborate* and write the definition on the lines below.

collaborate _____

What is the origin from List 5? _____

EST _____

EST _____

EST _____

Lesson Nine

10 Lesson Ten: More on the Farm

A. VERB STEM REVIEW

We already know that verb endings are attached to a part of the verb called the *present stem*. Fill in the blanks about how to find the present stem.

In order to find the present stem, you must remove the ending _____ from the second

principal part of the verb. The second principal part of the verb is called the _____ .

Write the present stem for the verb *laboro, -are* on the blank: _____

B. COMMANDS

The present stem also has another use as an *imperative*, or command. If you want to command one person to work, you would use the present stem of the verb *laboro*. Study the examples below:

Singular commands: Labōrā. *Work.*   Tondē. *Shear.*   Mulgē. *Milk.*

Translate the commands below that Grandfather gives to the children and Saxum.

(To Julius): Labōrā in agrō.   _____

(To Julia): Tondē agnum.   _____

(To Saxum): Mulgē vaccam.   _____

Puer potat.

When a command is given to more than one person, the ending **-te** must be added to the verb stem. Study the plural examples below:

Plural Commands: Labōrāte. *Work.*   Tondēte. *Shear.*   Mulgēte. *Milk.*

N.B. The implied subject of a command is *you* or *you all*.

Now suppose that the children and Saxum have brought friends to help at the farm. Translate these plural commands that Grandfather gives.

(To Julius and friends): Labōrāte in horreō. _____

(To Julia and friends): Tondēte agnōs. _____

(To Saxum and friends): Mulgēte caprās. _____

C. PRACTICE

Give these singular and plural commands in Latin. One example is done for you.

SINGULAR COMMANDS

1. *Crow.* ____Canā.____
2. *Drink.* _____
3. *Plow.* _____
4. *Cut.* _____

PLURAL COMMANDS

1. *Crow.* ____Canāte.____
2. *Drink.* _____
3. *Plow.* _____
4. *Cut.* _____

D. POSSUM AND INFINITIVE REVIEW

Label and translate the following sentences. <u>Underline</u> endings. Use the abbreviation INF when labeling infinitives.

1. Vacca potest potāre. _____

_____

2. Possumus labōrāre. _____

_____

Challenge Sentence: Non potes secāre faenum in prātō. _____

_____

6 List Six: Work on the Farm

VOCABULARY

Memorize the following Latin words and their translations. Also learn the genitive endings for nouns and the second principal parts for verbs.

Word	Derivative	Translation
1. olīva, -ae	_____	*olive, olive tree*
2. oleum, -ī	_____	*olive oil*
3. ūva, -ae	_____	*grape*
4. bacca, -ae	_____	*berry*
5. lūcus, -ī	_____	*grove*
6. hortus, -ī	_____	*garden*
7. rāmus, -ī	_____	*branch*
8. cavum, -ī	_____	*hole*
9. quālus, -ī	_____	*basket*
10. ampulla, -ae	_____	*flask, bottle*
11. fodicō, -āre	_____	*dig*
12. floreō, -ēre	_____	*bloom, flourish*
13. putō, -āre	_____	*prune*
14. compleō, -ēre	_____	*fill up*
15. cum	_____	*with* (preposition w/abl.)

List Six 73

REVIEW WORDS

1. pāla, -ae — *shovel*
2. herba, -ae — *plant*
3. pōmārium, -ī — *orchard*
4. mālum, -ī — *apple*
5. vīnea, -ae — *vineyard*
6. avia, -ae — *grandmother*
7. lībō, -āre — *sip, taste*
8. pōtō, -āre — *drink*
9. vīnum, -ī — *wine*
10. terra, -ae — *land, earth*

DŪCŌ CHANT

Here is a new verb chant to learn. It is an example of a third conjugation verb and means *lead*. Practice writing the *Dūco Chant* in the blank box below.

DŪCŌ CHANT – THIRD CONJUGATION

dūcō	dūcimus
dūcis	dūcitis
dūcit	dūcunt

11 Lesson Eleven: Work on the Farm

A. REVIEW INFINITIVES

An infinitive is the _____ principal part of the verb.

An infinitive ends in _____ . The infinitive ending means _____ .

Translate these infinitives from List 6:

1. complēre _____

2. fodicāre _____

3. florēre _____

4. putāre _____

B. REVIEW IMPERATIVES (COMMANDS)

The verb stem can also be used as a singular command. The verb stem is found by removing the **-re** from the infinitive. Translate these singular commands (commands to one person):

1. Complē. _____

2. Fodicā. _____

3. Florē. _____

4. Putā. _____

Sunt _____

To make a plural command, add -te to the verb stem. Translate these plural commands:

1. Complēte. _____

2. Fodicāte. _____

3. Florēte. _____

4. Putāte. _____

C. QUESTIONS

In English we make an *interrogative* sentence, or question, by placing a question mark at the end of the sentence. In Latin, the ending *-ne* is added to the first word in the sentence. Usually, the first word in a Latin question is the verb. Study the examples below.

    V-t SN DO
Ara<u>t</u>ne avus hortum?   *Does grandfather plow the garden?*
                                  (Is grandfather plowing the garden?)

    V-t   SN   DO
Liba<u>bunt</u>ne porcelli baccas?   *Will the little pigs taste the berries?*

    V-t   DO
Mulge<u>bas</u>ne vaccam?   *Were you milking the cow?*

N.B. Use helping verbs to begin your translation of Latin questions into English.

If the verb has a present tense ending, choose from *am, is, are, do, does*.
If the verb has a future tense ending, choose *will*.
If the verb has an imperfect tense ending, choose *was* or *were*.

In the examples above, the *-ne* ending is placed on the verb. While the verb is frequently the first word in a Latin question, other words are sometimes first. Consider this example:

  SN   DO V-t
Avusne hortum arat?   *Does grandfather plow the garden?*

The question is translated in the same way even though the *subject noun* is the first word in the sentence.

In the examples below, highlight the question ending and label parts of speech. Then translate these questions.

Porcellīne baccās libābunt? _____

_____

Vaccamne mulgēs? _____

_____

D. DERIVATIVE DIGGING

A question is called an *interrogative* statement. The word *interrogative* is a derivative of a Latin word we have already learned. What Latin word does *interrogative* come from?

_____

Lesson Eleven 77

12 Lesson Twelve: Work on the Farm

A. QUESTION REVIEW

1. What is the ending used to indicate a question in Latin? _____

2. To which word in the sentence is the question ending added? Underline the correct answer.

   first   *second*   *third*   *last*

3. Usually, which word is first in a Latin question? Underline the correct answer.

   direct object   *verb*   *subject noun*   *infinitive*

B. "IN A NUTSHELL"

When people want to summarize material in a short, easy way they sometimes use the expression "in a nutshell." A nutshell is not very large, so it cannot hold too much information. Here is a Latin nutshell to help you remember the endings **-ne**, **-re**, and **-te**.

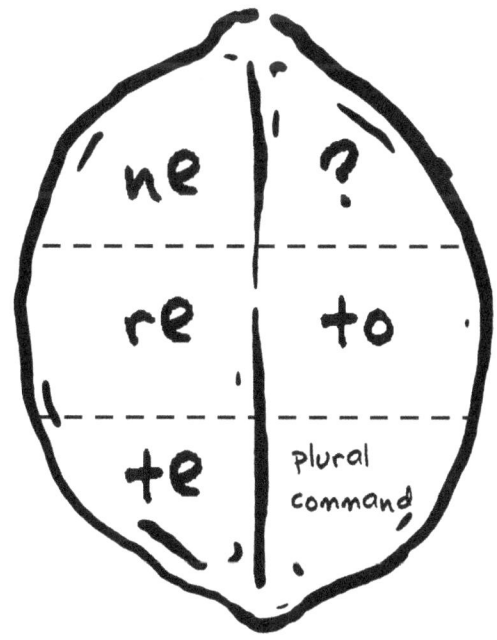

Lesson Twelve 79

C. THE PREPOSITION "CUM"

The word *cum* means "with". When *cum* is used in a sentence, its object of the preposition is always in the **ablative case**. Study the examples of sentences using *cum*:

    Iūlius ambulat cum amīcō.   *Julius walks with a friend.*

    Iūlia fodicat in horto cum porcā.*   *Julia digs in the garden with a female pig.*

*The DVD uses a different sentence as the second example.

D. TRANSLATION

Translate the following questions. <u>Underline</u> endings and label parts of speech. Remember to begin your translations with the correct helping verb.

1. Fodicatne Iūlius cum amīcō? _____

2. Complēbatne Iūlia qualum cum amicīs? _____

3. Aviane tondēbit capram cum Saxō? _____

4. Putatne avus rāmum? _____

5. Ambulābantne līberī in lūcum cum amīcīs? _____

6. Floretne hortus? _____

Lesson Twelve

Challenge: For fun, use complete sentences to answer one or more of these questions in Latin. Sentence #1 is done as an example.

1. <u>Iūlius fodicat cum amicō.</u>
2. _____
3. _____
4. _____
5. _____
6. _____

Puer fodicat terram.

Lesson Twelve 81

Unit Two Review

A. VOCABULARY

From memory, translate as many of these vocabulary words as you can. Then look up any you don't remember.

1. vacca, -ae _____

2. dō, -āre _____

3. faenum, -ī _____

4. horreum, -ī _____

5. possum, posse _____

6. secō, -āre _____

7. arō, -āre _____

8. ovis, ovis _____

9. agnus, -ī _____

10. porcellus, -ī _____

11. potō, -āre _____

12. ager, agrī _____

13. iuvō, -āre _____

14. oleum, -ī _____

15. hortus, -ī _____

16. ampulla, -ae   _____

17. quālus, -ī   _____

18. putō, -āre   _____

19. compleō, -ēre   _____

20. cum   _____

B. CHANT REVIEW

Fill in the following chants:

SECOND DECLENSION NEUTER

Case	Singular	Plural
Nom.	-um	
Gen.		
Dat.		
Acc.		
Abl.		

POSSUM CHANT

Conjugate the verb *possum* and give meanings:

possum - *I am able*	

DŪCŌ CHANT

Conjugate the verb *dūco*. You do not have to give meanings, but do spell correctly.

dūcō -	

C. INFINITIVES

Translate these infinitives, underline the verb stems and then tell whether they are first or second conjugation.

        TRANSLATION   CONJUGATION

1. putāre _____ _____

2. mulgēre _____ _____

D. INFINITIVE TRANSLATION

Translate these sentences containing infinitives:

1. Possum laborāre in hortō. _____

_____

2. Agricola potest putāre ramōs. _____

_____

Challenge Sentence: Iūlius et Iūlia possunt putāre vineās? _____

_____

Unit 2 Review

E. COMMAND TRANSLATION

Translate the following commands and tell whether they are singular or plural.

1. Fodicā cavum. _____

    Singular or plural? _____

2. Potāte aquam. _____

    Singular or plural? _____

3. Mulgē vaccam. _____

    Singular or plural? _____

F. QUESTION TRANSLATION

Translate the following questions. **Helpful Hint:** Begin your question with the correct helping verb.

1. Laborābantne līberī in horreō? _____

_____

2. Tondēbitne Saxum agnum? _____

_____

3. Hortusne floret? _____

4. Potātisne aquam? _____

_____

G. DERIVATIVES

From what Latin words do these English derivatives come? Derivatives are from Lists 4, 5, and 6.

DERIVATIVE	LATIN ORIGIN
1. pomander	_____
2. donate	_____
3. porcine	_____
4. cure	_____
5. aquarium	_____
6. horticulture	_____

Choose one derivative from above, look it up in an English dictionary, and write its meaning on the lines below:

Derivative: _____

Meaning: _____

Unit 2 Review

List Seven: A Visit to Rome

VOCABULARY

Memorize the following Latin words and their translations. Be sure to learn the genitive forms for nouns and the second principal parts for verbs.

Word	Derivative	Translation
1. Rōma,-ae	_____	*Rome*
2. urbs, urbis	_____	*city*
3. forum,-ī	_____	*public square*
4. aedificium,-ī	_____	*building*
5. templum,-ī	_____	*temple*
6. ecclēsia,-ae	_____	*church*
7. agentaria,-ae	_____	*bank*
8. columna,-ae	_____	*column*
9. monumentum,-ī	_____	*monument*
10. statua,-ae	_____	*statue*
11. via,-ae	_____	*street, road, way*
12. thermopōlium,-ī	_____	*hot food shop*
13. stō,-āre	_____	*stand*
14. exclāmō,-āre	_____	*exclaim*
15. errō, -āre	_____	*wander, err*

List Seven 89

REVIEW WORDS

1. spectō, -āre — *look at, watch*
2. ambulō, -āre — *walk*
3. laudō, -āre — *praise*
4. visitō, -āre — *visit*
5. cēna, -ae — *dinner, meal*
6. puer, -ī — *boy*
7. pecūnia, -ae — *money*
8. frāter, fratris — *brother*
9. pater, patris — *father*
10. portō, -āre — *carry*
11. numerō, -āre — *count*
12. monstro, -are — *show, point out*

AUDIŌ CHANT

Below is an example of a fourth conjugation verb. Start memorizing this new chant by copying it into the blank box below. *Audiō* means "I hear." This chant will follow the *Dūcō Chant*.

AUDIŌ CHANT – FOURTH CONJUGATION

audiō	audīmus
audīs	audītis
audit	audiunt

List Seven

13 Lesson Thirteen: A Visit to Rome

A. GENITIVE CASE . . . SHOWS DECLENSION

The genitive noun case is extremely important in Latin. Highlight or circle the genitive case endings in the chants below:

FIRST DECLENSION

Nom.	-a	-ae
Gen.	-ae	-ārum
Dat.	-ae	-īs
Acc.	-am	-ās
Abl.	-ā	-īs

SECOND DECLENSION

Nom.	-us	-ī
Gen.	-ī	-ōrum
Dat.	-ō	-īs
Acc.	-um	-ōs
Abl.	-ō	-īs

SECOND DECLENSION NEUTER

Nom.	-um	-a
Gen.	-ī	-ōrum
Dat.	-ō	-īs
Acc.	-um	-a
Abl.	-ō	-īs

The genitive case can tell us what declension (noun family) a word is from. The nominative case cannot always do that.

For example, the word **puer** is actually in the "Us" Family or second declension, even though its nominative form, *puer*, ends in **-er**. On a word list or in a Latin dictionary, the genitive form will be given as well: *puer, -ī*.

We know the word is second declension because nouns from that family have a genitive singular ending of **-ī**.

Answer the following questions by putting the correct declension number on the blank (1st, 2nd, 2nd N).

What declension has **-ae** for its genitive singular ending? _____

What declension has **-ī** for its genitive singular ending? _____ or _____

Draw a red circle around other case endings that look like the genitive endings on the declension charts above.

B. GENITIVE CASE . . . SHOWS THE BASE OF NOUNS

The genitive case can also help us find the base of a noun. Just as verbs have a stem to which endings are attached, so nouns have a base to which noun endings are attached. Here is a jingle to help you remember how to find the base of a noun:

Don't try to change the case until you find the base.
The genitive case is the place to find the base.

In order to find the base, you must use the genitive form of the word and remove the genitive ending. Then you may add other case endings, such as the accusative singular or the nominative plural. Study the examples below:

Nominative Word	Genitive Form	Base
via	viae	vi-
ventus	ventī	vent-
templum	templī	templ-

Try writing the base for the words below by removing the genitive ending.

Roma	Romae	_____
porcellus	porcellī	_____
forum	forī	_____

Lesson Thirteen

C. GENITIVE CASE . . . SHOWS POSSESSION

Finally, the genitive case can show possession, or ownership. In English, we show that a noun is possessive by using an apostrophe. Where does the apostrophe go if the possessive noun is singular (before the *s* or after the *s*)? Where does it go if the possessive noun is plural? Consider the possessive noun examples below and highlight the genitive endings on the Latin possessive nouns.

    the girl's chair   *sella puellae*
    the boy student's book   *liber discipulī*

Here are some genitive plural examples. Highlight the genitive endings on the possessive nouns.

    the girls' chair   *sella puellārum*
    the boy students' book   *liber discipulōrum*

N.B. Notice that possessive nouns can come *after* the noun they go with.

Quid est?
Est _____

Lesson Thirteen

Try translating these phrases containing possessive nouns in the genitive case:

1. statua templī   _____

2. cēna porcellī   _____

3. via Romae   _____

Challenge: viae Romae   _____

D. DERIVATIVE DIGGING

What book in the Bible is a derivative of the Latin word *ecclēsia*?

_____

Forum Romae!

14 Lesson Fourteen: A Visit to Rome

A. VERB STEM REVIEW

Underline the stems of the following verbs.

1. monstrāre
2. exclamāre
3. numerāre

B. JINGLE REVIEW

Fill in the blanks on the jingle below:

Don't try to change the _____

Until you find the _____

The _____ *case is the place to find the* _____ .

For the nouns below, both the nominative and genitive cases are given. Underline the base of each noun:

NOMINATIVE	GENITIVE
Rōma	Rōmae
monumentum	monumentī
statua	statuae
circus	circī
aedificium	aedificiī
puer	puerī

C. TRANSLATION

Translate the sentences below. Each sentence contains a possessive noun. Underline endings and label parts of speech. The label for possessive nouns is PNA (Possessive Noun Adjective).

Helpful Hint: Find the verb first! Next, look for a subject noun to go with the verb. Then check to see if a direct object or possessive noun is present. The first sentence is done as an example.

```
   CSN  C  CSN    V-t     P  OP   PNA
```
1. Līber**ī** et Sax**um** ambula**nt** in vi**īs** Rom**ae**. *The children and Saxum (Rock) walk in Rome's streets.*

2. Iūlius columnās ecclēsiae monstrat. _____

3. Iūlia et Claudia statuam templī laudant. _____

4. Saxum monumenta Romae amat! _____

5. Pater Iūlī pecuniam portat ad agentariam. _____

6. Vir pecuniam patris* numerat in agentariā. _____

7. Pater liberōrum ambulat ad thermopolium. _____

Patris is the genitive form of *pater*. It is from the third declension, which is introduced with List 16.

Lesson Fourteen

D. TIDBIT

A *thermopolium* was a hot food shop. Holes in a counter held jars of hot food or wine. Since most Romans could not afford to have a kitchen they would often buy food at one of the *thermopolia*. The thermopolium has been compared to modern day fast food restaurants.

Quid est?
Est _____

Lesson Fourteen 97

8 List Eight: Birthday Party

A. VOCABULARY

Memorize the following Latin words and their translations.

Word	Derivative	Translation
1. dies nātālis		*birthday*
2. dōnum, -ī		*gift*
3. convīvium, -ī		*party*
4. lībum nātāle		*birthday cake*
5. mappa, -ae		*napkin*
6. stomachus, -ī		*stomach*
7. candēla, -ae		*candle*
8. fūmus, -ī		*smoke*
9. annus, -ī		*year*
10. aeger, aegra, aegrum		*sick*
11. saltō, -āre		*dance*
12. flō, -āre		*blow*
13. ornō, -āre		*decorate, equip*
14. occultō, -āre		*hide*
15. celebrō, -āre		*celebrate*

REVIEW WORDS

1. do, -āre — *give*
2. habeō, -ēre — *have, hold*
3. parō, -āre — *prepare*
4. secō, -āre — *cut*
5. numerō, -āre — *count*
6. cantō, -āre — *sing*
7. Review of cardinal numbers:
   - ūnus - *one*
   - duo - *two*
   - trēs - *three*
   - quattuor - *four*
   - quīnque - *five*
   - sex - *six*
   - septem - *seven*
   - octō - *eight*
   - novem - *nine*
   - decem - *ten*

Claudius celebrat diem natalis.

List Eight

15 Lesson Fifteen: Birthday Party

A. GENITIVE REVIEW

There are three ways to use the genitive case:

1. Identify the declension
2. Find the base of a noun
3. Use as a possessive noun

Write the correct genitive endings on the blanks below. Use your noun chant charts to help you.

	GENITIVE SINGULAR	GENITIVE PLURAL
First Declension	_____	_____
Second Declension	_____	_____
Second Dec. Neuter	_____	_____

B. NOUN REVIEW

Find the base of these nouns by removing the genitive singular ending and write the base on the line.

	BASE
1. convīvium, -ī	_____
2. fūmus, -ī	_____
3. candēla, -ae	_____

C. TRANSLATION

Translate the sentences below. <u>Underline</u> endings and label parts of speech. Some sentences contain possessive nouns.

1. Iūlius diem nātālem habēbit. _____

2. Amīcī Iūliae ornābunt. _____

3. Iūlia dōnum frātris* occultābit. _____

4. Saxum apportābit lībum nātāle Iūlī _____

Frātris is the genitive form of *frāter*.

D. DERIVATIVE DIGGING

Choose one derivative from this week's list. Look your derivative up in an English dictionary and write its definition (meaning) on the lines below. Also give its Latin origin (the Latin word it comes from). Finally, use your derivative in a sentence.

Derivative: _____

Definition: _____

Latin origin: _____

Sentence: _____

Lesson Fifteen

16 Lesson Sixteen: Birthday Party

A. DATIVE CASE AND INDIRECT OBJECTS

Highlight the dative endings in the noun chants below.

FIRST DECLENSION

Nom.	-a	-ae
Gen.	-ae	-ārum
Dat.	-ae	-īs
Acc.	-am	-ās
Abl.	-ā	-īs

SECOND DECLENSION

Nom.	-us	-ī
Gen.	-ī	-ōrum
Dat.	-ō	-īs
Acc.	-um	-ōs
Abl.	-ō	-īs

SECOND DECLENSION NEUTER

Nom.	-um	-a
Gen.	-ī	-ōrum
Dat.	-ō	-īs
Acc.	-um	-a
Abl.	-ō	-īs

Quid est?
Est _____

Lesson Sixteen 103

B. SENTENCE PATTERNS

Label and translate the following sentences and identify the pattern.
(Pattern 1=SN, V; Pattern 2=SN, V-t, DO)

PATTERN

1. Iūlia dat. _____ _____

2. Iūlia dōnum dat. _____ _____

PATTERN 3 SENTENCES

Now look at the Pattern 3 sentence below. Pattern 3 adds an *indirect object*. Indirect objects usually name a person or thing **to whom** something is given or **for whom** something is done. <u>Underline</u> the endings on the Pattern 3 sentence below and then answer the questions about it.

    SN **IO** DO V-t   SN V-t **IO** DO
    Iūli<u>a</u> **Iūli<u>ō</u>** dōn<u>um</u> da<u>t</u>.   *Julia gives **Julius** a gift.*

What does Julia give? _____

What part of speech is it? _____

Who does she give it to? _____

What part of speech is it? _____

C. MATCHING

Draw lines between the part of speech and its case:

    Subject Noun   dative case

    Possessive Noun   accusative case

    Direct Object   nominative case

    Indirect Object   genitive case

D. TRANSLATION

Translate the following sentences. Underline endings and label parts of speech.

1. Iūlius dat. _____

2. Iūlius candēlam dat. _____

3. Iūlius Iūliae candēlam dat. _____

_____

Challenge sentence: (Also contains a possessive noun) Iūlius Iūliae candēlam Saxī dat.

_____

Fūmus flat ad Iūlium.

Lesson Sixteen 105

9 List Nine: Illness

A. VOCABULARY

Memorize the following Latin words and their translations. Also learn genitive endings for nouns and second principal parts for verbs.

Word	Derivative	Translation
1. frūstum, -ī	_____	*piece*
2. medicus, -ī	_____	*doctor*
3. medicāmentum, -ī	_____	*medicine*
4. morbus, -ī	_____	*sickness*
5. dolor stomachī	_____	*stomach ache*
6. pilula, -ae	_____	*pill*
7. lectus, -ī	_____	*bed*
8. lingua, -ae	_____	*tongue*
9. aegrōtō, -āre	_____	*be sick*
10. doleō, -ēre	_____	*grieve*
11. cubō, -āre	_____	*lie down*
12. dēvorō, -āre	_____	*swallow*
13. moneō, -ēre	_____	*warn*
14. ostendē	_____	*stick out* (command)
15. quod	_____	*because*

REVIEW WORDS

1. lībum nātāle — *birthday cake*
2. ampulla, -ae — *flask, bottle*
3. quīnque — *five*
4. habeō, -ēre — *have, hold*
5. monstrō, -āre — *show*
6. libō, -āre — *taste, sip*
7. dō, -āre — *give*
8. parō, -āre — *prepare*
9. nōn — *no, nor not*
10. cum (w/abl.) — *with*
11. in (w/abl.) — *in or on*
12. narrō, -āre — *tell, say*
13. domus, -us — *house, home*

B. THIRD DECLENSION CHANT

Memorize and copy the new noun chant below. It is called Third Declension. This chant will follow second declension neuter.

THIRD DECLENSION

Nom.	-x	-ēs
Gen.	-is	-um
Dat.	-ī	-ibus
Acc.	-em	-ēs
Abl.	-e	-ibus

Nom.		
Gen.		
Dat.		
Acc.		
Abl.		

List Nine

17 Lesson Seventeen: Illness

A. NOUN CASE REVIEW

Fill in the blanks below with the correct noun case. Choose from *nominative, genitive, dative,* and *accusative.*

1. The **subject noun** goes in the _____ case.

2. The **direct object** goes in the _____ case.

3. The **possessive noun** goes in the _____ case.

4. The **indirect object** goes in the _____ case.

B. TRANSLATION

Label parts of speech and translate these sentences into Latin. Remember to use the correct case endings! See section A above to remind you of which case goes with each part of speech.

1. The doctor gives. _____

2. The doctor gives medicine. _____

3. The doctor gives Julius medicine. _____

4. The doctor gives Julius Julia's medicine. _____

Challenge sentence: Does the doctor give Julia Julius's medicine? _____

C. REVIEW

What case is used to find the base of a noun? _____

Write the **base** of the following nouns.

1. medicus, -ī _____

2. pilula, -ae _____

3. frūstum, -ī _____

D. DERIVATIVE DIGGING

Look up the following English derivatives in a dictionary and write their meanings on the lines provided. Both words come from the Latin word *doleō*.

doleful - _____

dolorous - _____

What other Latin word on List 9 is related to *doleō*? _____

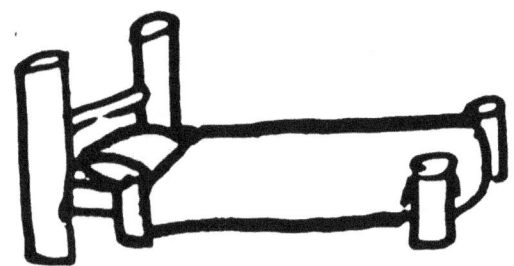

Quid est?
Est _____

Lesson Seventeen

18 Lesson Eighteen: Illness

A. GENITIVE CASE REVIEW

Put genitive singular endings on the following nouns and then translate the **genitive forms**. The first one is done as an example.

Nominative	Genitive Singular	Translation
1. medicus	medicī	the doctor's
2. lingua		
3. frūstrum		

Now put genitive plural endings on these nouns and translate. The first one is done for you.

Nominative	Genitive Plural	Translation
1. medicus	medicōrum	the doctors'
2. statua		
3. templum		

Case	Singular	Plural
Nom.	-us	-ī
Gen.	-ī	-ōrum
Dat.	-ō	-īs
Acc.	-um	-ōs
Abl.	-ō	-īs

B. DATIVE CASE REVIEW

Put the dative singular endings on the following nouns. You do not have to translate these. The first one is done for you.

Nominative	Dative Singular	Dative Plural
1. medicus	medicō	medicīs
2. ecclēsia		
3. Saxum		

Case	Singular	Plural
Nom.	-us	-ī
Gen.	-ī	-ōrum
Dat.	-ō	-īs
Acc.	-um	-ōs
Abl.	-ō	-īs

C. TRANSLATION

Label and translate the sentences below. <u>Underline endings.</u> Many sentences contain possessive nouns.

Possessive nouns go in the _____ case.

1. Iūlius et Iūlia aegrotant. _____

2. Medicus vīsitat domum liberōrum. _____

3. Medicus linguam Iūliae spectat. _____

4. Iulius pilulam medicī devorat. _____

Lesson Eighteen

D. MORE TRANSLATION

Label and translate these sentences. <u>Underline endings</u>. Some sentences contain indirect objects. .

Indirect objects go in the _____ case.

1. Iūlius amābat lībum nātāle. _____

2. Iūlius habēbat dolorem* stomachī quod quīnque frusta devorābat! _____
_____

3. Māter Iūliō medicāmentum dat. _____

4. Medicus Iūliō narrat, "Ostendē linguam." _____
_____

5. Iūlius medicō linguam mōnstrat. _____

*dolorem is the accusative singular of dolor.

Quid est?
Est _____

Lesson Eighteen 113

E. TIDBIT

Roman doctors were always men. Some doctors came from Greece. They carried tools with them, many of which resemble tools doctors still use today, such as the scalpel. Tools were boiled in water before use. Women might act as midwives to help deliver babies. Most medicines were made from herbs.

114 Lesson Eighteen

Unit Three Review

A. VOCABULARY

From memory, translate as many of these vocabulary words as you can. Then look up any you don't remember. The last five words are in English and you must give the correct Latin word.

1. urbs, urbis _____

2. ecclēsia, -ae _____

3. via, -ae _____

4. errō, -āre _____

5. stō, -āre _____

6. dōnum, -ī _____

7. annus, -ī _____

8. occultō, -āre _____

9. aeger, aegra, aegrum _____

10. convīvium, -ī _____

11. lectus, -ī _____

12. morbus, -ī _____

13. moneō, -ēre _____

14. quod _____

15. lingua, -ae _____

English to Latin

16. doctor _____

17. grieve _____

18. smoke _____

19. decorate, equip _____

20. public square _____

B. CHANT REVIEW

Fill in the chants below:

AUDIO CHANT

audio	

THIRD DECLENSION

-x	

C. NOUN CASE REVIEW

What case do they go in? Fill in the blank with the correct case for each part of speech.

1. subject noun - _____

2. direct object - _____

3. possessive noun - _____

4. indirect object - _____

D. TRANSLATION

Label and translate the following sentences. <u>Underline</u> endings.

1. Iūlia visitābit. _____

2. Iūlia visitābit Rōmam. _____

3. Iūlia visitābit forum Rōmae. _____

_____

4. Iūlia et Saxum dant. _____

5. Iūlia et Saxum dōnum dant. _____

6. Iūlia et Saxum Iūliō dōnum dant. _____

_____

7. Māter lībum nātāle Iūlī parābat. _____

8. Quattuor līberī saltant et celebrant in forō. _____

_____

9. Iūlius cubābat in lectō quod aegrotābat. _____

_____

10. Soror Iūlī dolēbat quod Iūlius morbum habēbat. _____

_____

11. Medicus Iūliō pilulās dat. _____

_____

E. VERB TRANSLATION

Translate the following verbs. <u>Underline</u> endings.

1. exclamābant _____

2. errābimus _____

3. stātis _____

4. saltābō _____

5. flābās _____

6. ornāmus _____

7. occultābit _____

8. celebrās _____

9. cubābātis _____

10. monēbam _____

F. DERIVATIVES

Give derivatives for the following Latin words.

1. lingua _____

2. devorō _____

3. morbus _____

4. dōnum _____

5. annus _____

6. ornō _____

7. urbs _____

8. via _____

9. errō _____

10. doleō _____

10 List Ten: Colors and Clothes

VOCABULARY

Memorize the following Latin words and their translations. Also learn the genitive endings for nouns, the second principal parts of verbs, and all three endings for adjectives.

WORD	DERIVATIVE	TRANSLATION
1. stola, -ae	_____	*dress*
2. palla, -ae	_____	*cloak*
3. toga, -ae	_____	*toga*
4. calceus, -ī	_____	*shoe*
5. textum, -ī	_____	*cloth*
6. coma, -ae	_____	*hair, leaves of a tree*
7. caeruleus, -a, -um	_____	*blue*
8. ruber, rubra, rubrum*	_____	*red*
9. flāvus, -a, -um	_____	*yellow, blond*
10. roseus, -a, -um	_____	*pink*
11. fulvus, -a, -um	_____	*brown*
12. albus, -a, -um	_____	*white*
13. niger, nigra, nigrum*	_____	*black*
14. magnus, -a, -um	_____	*large*
15. parvus, -a, -um	_____	*small, little*

*Just as some second declension nouns end in **-er** in the nominative singular, so do some adjectives.

REVIEW WORDS

1. globulus, -ī   *button*
2. tunica, -ae   *tunic*
3. pilula, -ae   *pill*
4. agnus, -ī   *lamb*
5. gestō, -āre   *wear*

THIRD DECLENSION I-STEM CHANT

Here is a new noun chant to learn. It is called Third Declension I-stem and it is a cousin of the regular Third Declension which you already know. The Third Declension I-stem follows Third Declension. Memorize and copy the new chant.

THIRD DECLENSION I-STEM

Nom.	-is	-ēs
Gen.	-is	-ium
Dat.	-ī	-ibus
Acc.	-em	-ēs
Abl.	-e	-ibus

Nom.		
Gen.		
Dat.		
Acc.		
Abl.		

Lesson Nineteen: Colors and Clothes

A. ADJECTIVES AND GENDER

Adjectives are words which describe nouns or pronouns. In Latin, an adjective often comes after the noun it describes. In English, we might say "the red dress" but in Latin we would say *stola rubra* (the dress red).

GENDER: Latin adjectives must match the nouns they describe in *gender*. *Gender* refers to whether a noun is masculine, feminine, or neuter. It is obvious that men, boys, and male animals are masculine. Women, girls, and female animals are feminine. But Latin differs from English when it comes to *things*. In English, we consider most things to be neuter (neither masculine or feminine). In English, a table is neuter, but in Latin a table (*mensa*) is considered feminine. So, in Latin, things can be feminine, masculine, or neuter.

In Latin, adjectives have three endings which represent the three genders. In the dictionary or on a word list, all three gender endings are given, as in the example below:

flavus, -a, -um

-us is masculine, **-a** is feminine, and **-um** is neuter. Each of these endings represents a declension.

FIRST DECLENSION (feminine)

-a	-ae
-ae	-ārum
-ae	-īs
-am	-ās
-ā	-īs

SECOND DECLENSION (masculine)

-us	-ī
-ī	-ōrum
-ō	-īs
-um	-ōs
-ō	-īs

SECOND DECLENSION NEUTER (neuter)

-um	-a
-ī	-ōrum
-ō	-īs
-um	-a
-ō	-īs

Nouns that end in **-us** in the nominative singular are almost always masculine; nouns that end in **-a** are usually feminine; nouns that end in **-um** are always neuter. Study the examples of noun-adjective phrases below and write the gender of each phrase on the blank.

calceus flāvus	*the yellow shoe*	_____
stola flāva	*the yellow dress*	_____
textum flāvum	*the yellow cloth*	_____

N.B. Some adjectives have a masculine ending of **-er** instead of **-us**.

B. TRANSLATION

Translate these noun-adjective phrases into English. On the small blank, tell the gender of each by abbreviating **m.** for masculine, **f.** for feminine, and **n.** for neuter.

1. palla rubra _____ _____
2. calceus fulvus _____ _____
3. globulus niger _____ _____
4. textum caeruleum _____ _____
5. toga alba _____ _____

C. TRANSLATE INTO LATIN

Now translate these noun-adjective phrases into Latin. Put the noun first and make the adjective match the noun in gender. An example is done for you.

1. An olive green dress — stola herbācea*
2. A black shoe — _____
3. A yellow cloth — _____

4. A red button _____

5. A pink cloak _____

*This word does not appear in our vocabulary list, but it is included in the glossary.

Quid est?
Est _____

D. DERIVATIVE DIGGING

Using List 10, try to answer the following derivative questions.

1. What do you call an all-white animal? _____

   What is the Latin origin for this derivative? _____

2. What African nation takes its name from the Latin word *niger*? _____

   Challenge: Why is *comet* a good name for this type of heavenly body? _____

   _____

Lesson Nineteen

Draw a picture of a comet below:

20 Lesson Twenty: Colors and Clothes

A. ADJECTIVES REVIEW

We have learned that adjectives must match the nouns they describe in gender. If a noun is masculine, the adjective describing it must be masculine. The same thing is true for feminine and neuter nouns. Above each box write the gender of the chant.

FIRST DECLENSION

-a	-ae
-ae	-ārum
-ae	-īs
-am	-ās
-ā	-īs

SECOND DECLENSION

-us	-ī
-ī	-ōrum
-ō	-īs
-um	-ōs
-ō	-īs

SECOND DEC. NEUT.

-um	-a
-ī	-ōrum
-ō	-īs
-um	-a
-ō	-īs

B. ADJECTIVES AND NUMBER

Adjectives must also match nouns in number. By number we mean singular or plural.

If a noun is singular, the adjective describing it must be singular. If a noun is plural, the adjective describing it must be plural. Study the examples below.

Singular: *pilula caerulea*   a blue pill
Plural: *pilulae caeruleae*   blue pills

Singular: *agnus albus*   a white lamb
Plural: *agnī albī*   white lambs

Singular: *pirum flāvum*   a yellow pear
Plural: *pira flāva**   yellow pears

*N.B. Be careful of the second declension neuter plural. At first glance, it looks like first declension singular! Also, please note that *pirum* is a List 22 vocabulary word.

C. TRANSLATION

Translate these noun-adjective phrases. Tell whether the phrase is singular or plural.

	NOUN-ADJECTIVE PHRASES	SINGULAR OR PLURAL?
1. palla nigra		
2. togae albae		
3. texta rubra		
4. calceī fulvī		
5. textum magnum		
6. agnus parvus		
7. equus niger		

D. TIDBIT

Roman men usually wore white or off-white garments, although a color, especially purple, might be worn by someone in an honored position. Senators had a purple border on their robes. Women's clothing was of different colors but the styles were very simple. Women were likely to dress up by wearing jewelry and having elaborate hairstyles.

11 List Eleven: A Visit to the Jewelry Store

A. VOCABULARY

Memorize the following Latin words and their translations. Learn the genitive forms for nouns and the second principal parts for verbs.

WORD	DERIVATIVE	TRANSLATION
1. armilla, -ae		*bracelet*
2. ānulus, -ī		*ring*
3. gemma, -ae		*jewel*
4. margarīta, -ae		*pearl*
5. aurum, -ī		*gold*
6. sīca, -ae		*dagger*
7. scūtum, -ī		*shield*
8. tabernārius, -ī		*shopkeeper*
9. longus, -a, -um		*long*
10. pulcher, pulchra, pulchrum		*beautiful, handsome*
11. foedus, -a, -um		*ugly*
12. acūtus, -a, -um		*sharp, intelligent*
13. venditō, -āre		*sell*
14. limō, -āre		*polish*
15. administrō, -āre		*help, assist*

REVIEW WORDS

1. luceō*, -ēre — *shine, be bright*
2. dō, -āre — *give*
3. monstrō, -āre — *show*
4. parō, -āre — *prepare*
5. taberna, -ae — *shop*
6. gladius*, -ī — *sword*
7. habeō, -ēre — *have, hold*

Gladius and *luceo* are from Logos Latin 1, but will also appear as vocabulary words for this year on Lists 21 and 22.

FOURTH DECLENSION CHANT

Memorize and copy the new noun chant. It is called Fourth Declension Chant.

FOURTH DECLENSION

-us	-ūs
-ūs	-uum
-uī	-ibus
-um	-ūs
-ū	-ibus

N.B. What other declension chant also begins with **-us**? Be careful not to confuse them.

List Eleven

21 Lesson Twenty-One: A Visit to the Jewelry Store

A. ADJECTIVE REVIEW

Fill in the blanks below:

1. Adjectives must match the nouns they describe in **gender**.

    What are the three genders?

    _____ , _____ , and _____ .

2. Adjectives must match the nouns they describe in **number**.

    What is meant by number?

    _____ or _____ .

B. ADJECTIVES AND CASE

A third way in which adjectives must match the nouns they describe is in case. If a noun is in the nominative case, then the adjective which describes it must also be nominative. If a noun is in the accusative case, then the adjective must also be accusative. For now, we will only work with adjectives in the nominative and accusative cases.

Fill in the missing noun cases: Nominative _____

  _____

  _____

  Accusative _____

  _____

In what case do subject nouns go? _____

In what case do direct objects go? _____

C. PRACTICE

Translate these noun-adjective phrases in the **nominative case**. The first one is done as an example. Label each one according to gender. Abbreviate using **m.** for masculine, **f.** for feminine and **n.** for neuter. Remember that adjectives often follow the noun they describe.

N-Adj PHRASE	TRANSLATION	GENDER
1. armilla foeda	ugly bracelet	f.
2. tabernārius acutus		
3. aurum pulchrum		
4. margarīta pulchra		
5. tabernāriī acutī		

In the phrases above, write the number of the one which is plural: _____

Now translate noun-adjective phrases in the accusative case. The first one is done as an example.

N-Adj PHRASE	TRANSLATION	GENDER
1. armillam foedam	ugly bracelet	f.
2. scūtum longum		
3. sīcam acutam		
4. ānulum pulchrum		
5. sīcas longās		

In the phrases above, which one is plural? _____

Lesson Twenty-One

D. TRANSLATION

Practice translations containing adjectives. Underline endings and label parts of speech. The first one is done as an example.

   SN   DO   Adj   V-t
1. Iūlia armillam pulchram gestabat. Julia was wearing a beautiful bracelet.

2. Tabernārius acūtus Iūliam administrat. _____

3. Claudia gemmas caeruleas amat. _____

4. Iūlius et Claudius ambulant ad tabernam magnam. _____

5. Tabernārius gladium longum limat. _____

6. Gladius pulcher lucet. _____

7. Puerī scūtum magnum habent. _____

E. TIDBIT

Roman women wore jewelry containing colorful glass beads or polished rocks, as well as pearls. These could adorn earrings, necklaces, bracelets, rings, clothing pins, or hair ornaments. Men wore only rings, usually just one, although there are reports of some wearing a ring on every finger!

22 Lesson Twenty-Two: A Visit to the Jewelry Store

A. ADJECTIVE REVIEW

Fill in the blanks about adjectives.

Adjectives match the nouns they describe in gender, number, and case.

What are the three genders?

_____ , _____ , and _____ .

What is meant by number? _____ or _____ .

What are the five noun cases? _____ , _____ ,

_____ , _____ , _____ .

Which case is used for indirect objects? _____

Which case is used for subject nouns? _____

Which case is used for possessive nouns? _____

Which case is used for direct objects? _____

B. TRANSLATION

Label and translate the following sentences. <u>Underline</u> endings. Some sentences contain indirect objects or possessive nouns.

1. Iūlius Iūliae margarītam pulchram dat. _____

_____

Lesson Twenty-Two

2. Iūlia Iūliō scūtum rubrum dat.

3. Iūlia Claudiō scūtum rubrum Iūlī monstrat.

4. Tabernārius magnus Claudiae anulōs venditat.

5. Iūlia non* amat armillam foedam.

* Use the correct helping verb with the adverb *non*.

C. DERIVATIVE DIGGING

The derivative *escutcheon* comes from the Latin word *scutum*. Look up *escutcheon* in a dictionary and write its definition on the lines below. Then draw a picture of an escutcheon.

escutcheon:

12 List Twelve: Trouble with the Shopkeeper

VOCABULARY

Memorize the following Latin words and their translations. Learn the genitive forms for nouns and the second principal parts for verbs. Know all three endings for adjectives.

WORD	DERIVATIVE	TRANSLATION
1. fenestra, -ae		*window*
2. pila, -ae		*ball*
3. mūrus, -ī		*wall*
4. campus, -ī		*athletic field, plain*
5. plaustrum, -ī		*cart, wagon*
6. īrātus, -a, -um		*angry*
7. lātus, -a, -um		*wide*
8. altus, -a, -um		*high, tall*
9. tardus, -a, -um		*slow*
10. citus, -a, -um		*fast, swift*
11. rotundus, -a, -um		*round*
12. iactō, -āre		*throw*
13. calcitrō, -āre		*kick*
14. clāmō, -āre		*shout*
15. per		*through* (preposition with accusative)

List Twelve 137

REVIEW WORDS

1. terra, -ae — *ground, land*
2. properō, -āre — *hurry*
3. equus, -ī — *horse*
4. equitō, -āre — *ride on horseback*
5. ambulō, -āre — *walk*
6. pugnō, -āre* — *fight*
7. dō, -āre — *give*
8. trans** — *across, over* (prep. w/acc.)
9. taberna, -ae — *shop*
10. tabernārius, -ī — *shopkeeper*
11. pecūnia, -ae — *money*
12. moveo, -ere — *move*

Pugno is from Logos Latin 1, but will also appear as a vocabulary word for this year on List 24.
**trans is a vocab. word from List 23.

FOURTH DECLENSION NEUTER CHANT

Learn the new noun chant below. It is called Fourth Declension Neuter and is a cousin of Fourth Declension.

FOURTH DECLENSION NEUTER

-ū	-ua
-ūs	-uum
-ū	-ibus
-ū	-ua
-ū	-ibus

Practice writing Fourth Declension Neuter in the box below:

List Twelve

23 Lesson Twenty-Three: Trouble with the Shopkeeper

A. REVIEW

Possum Review: Conjugate (put endings on) the Possum Chant and translate.

PERSON	SINGULAR	PLURAL
1st	possum - *I am able*	
2nd		
3rd		

Infinitive Review: Write and translate the infinitives for verbs from List 12. The first one is done for you.

VERB	INFINITIVE	TRANSLATION OF INFINITIVE
1. iactō	iactāre	to throw
2. calcitrō	_____	_____
3. clamō	_____	_____

Adjective Review: Tell the gender of the endings below. Are they masculine, feminine, or neuter?

	GENDER
1. -us	_____
2. -a	_____
3. -um	_____

Lesson Twenty-Three 139

B. PRACTICE

Translate these English adjectives into Latin. All are in the nominative case. Pay attention to the **gender** of the noun and use the correct adjective ending. One is done as an example.

1. round ball   *pila*   rotunda

2. wide athletic field   *campus*   _____

3. swift cart   *plaustrum* _____

4. round windows   *fenestrae* _____

5. high walls   *mūrī*   _____

C. TRANSLATION

Label and translate the following sentences. Underline endings on nouns, verbs, and adjectives. Labels to choose from: SN, V, V-t, INF, DO, IO, PNA, P, OP, Adj. The first sentence is done for you.

```
   SN    V    INF    DO   Adj.   P    OP
```
1. Iūli<u>us</u> potes<u>t</u> calcitrā<u>re</u> pil<u>am</u> rotund<u>am</u> trans camp<u>um</u>.   Julius is able to kick the round ball across the plain (or athletic field).

2. Claudius pilam iactat per fenestram altam in tabernā! _____

3. Tabernārius īrātus clamat. _____

4. Claudius tabernāriō pēcuniam dat. _____

5. Puellae (Iūlia et Claudia) ambulant trans* campum lātum. _____

6. Saxum equitat per tabernam tabernī. _____

7. Tabernārius īrātus trans* mūrum altum Saxum iactat. _____

*_Trans_ appears in a later vocabulary list (23), but it is also in the glossary.

D. DERIVATIVE DIGGING

Look up the English derivative *eject* and write its meaning on the lines below. What Latin word does this come from? **Hint:** Remember that the letter *i* at the beginning of a Latin word later became a *j*.

_____

_____

_____

24 Lesson Twenty-Four: Trouble with the Shopkeeper

A. QUESTION REVIEW

Fill in the blanks about Latin questions:

To form a Latin question, the ending _____ is added to the first word in the sentence.

Usually, the first word in a Latin question is the _____ .

Label and translate these questions into English. Remember to start with the correct helping verb.

1. Venditatne tabernārius margarītam? _____

_____

2. Iactābuntne Saxum et Iulius pilam? _____

_____

3. Clamābāmusne? _____

_____

B. VERB REVIEW

List the helping verbs for these verb tenses.

Present Tense   _____ , _____ , _____ , _____ , _____

Imperfect Tense   _____ , _____ , _____

Future Tense   _____

Underline verb endings and translate the verbs below:

1. calcitrant _____

2. iactābō _____

3. clamābāmus _____

4. vendītābit _____

5. līmābās _____

6. administrātis _____

7. calcitrābitis _____

8. iactāmus _____

9. clamat _____

10. vendītābam _____

C. TRANSLATION

Label and translate the following sentences. Underline endings on nouns and verbs.

1. Iūlia cita et Iūlius citus properābant trans campum. _____

_____

2. Iūlia Iūliō pilam rotundam iactat. _____

_____

3. Iūlius pilam calcitrat in plaustrum tardum.* _____

_____

4. Agricola plaustrum tardum movēbat per murum altum. _____

_____

Lesson Twenty-Four

5. Līberī rogant: "Iactābisne pilam?" _____

6. Agricola pilam iactat trans mūrum altum. _____

*N.B. Remember, the Latin preposition **in** means *into* when the object of preposition is in the accusative case.

D. TIDBIT

The Romans enjoyed many games involving balls. Balls could be filled with hair, feathers or air.

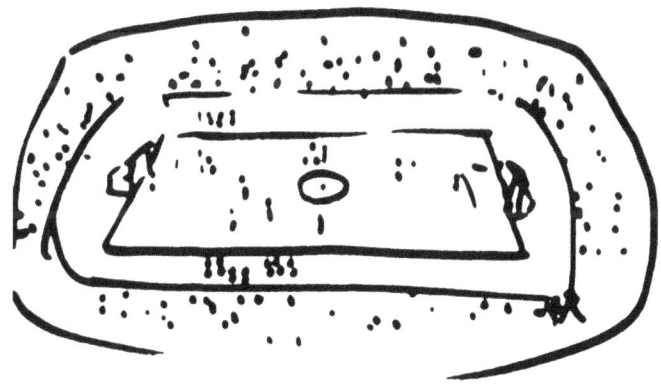

Unit Four Review

A. VOCABULARY

From memory, translate as many of these vocabulary words as you can. Then look up any you don't remember.

1. stola, -ae _____

2. ānulus, -ī _____

3. mūrus, -ī _____

4. calceus, ī _____

5. aurum, -ī _____

6. īrātus, -a, -um _____

7. caeruleus, -a, -um _____

8. tabernārius, -ī _____

9. tardus, -a, -um _____

10. roseus, -a, -um _____

11. foedus, -a, -um _____

12. per _____

13. niger, nigra, nigrum _____

14. armilla, -ae _____

15. pila, -ae _____

English to Latin

16. cloth   _____

17. dagger   _____

18. high, tall   _____

19. small   _____

20. window   _____

B. CHANT REVIEW

Fill in the chants below:

THIRD DECLENSION

-x	
-is	

THIRD DECLENSION I-STEM

-is	
-is	

FOURTH DECLENSION

-us	
-ūs	

FOURTH DECLENSION NEUTER

-ū	
-ūs	

C. ADJECTIVES

Choose from the following terms to correctly fill in the blanks about the ways adjectives must match the nouns they describe: *number, ablative, feminine, accusative, case, singular, gender, masculine, plural, neuter, dative, genitive, nominative.*

1. In what three ways must adjectives match the nouns they describe?

_____ , _____ , and _____ .

2. What are the three genders?

_____ , _____ , and _____ .

3. Which gender uses the **-us** chant? _____

4. Which gender uses the **-a** chant? _____

5. Which gender use the **-um** chant? _____

6. What terms refer to number? _____ and _____ .

7. What are the five noun cases in order? _____ , _____ , _____ , _____ , _____ .

Unit 4 Review

D. TRANSLATION

Translate the following verbs. <u>Underline</u> endings.

1. iactātis _____

2. calcitrābunt _____

3. clamābāmus _____

4. venditābō _____

5. līmābit _____

6. administrās _____

Now translate these English verbs into Latin.

1. I was kicking. _____

2. We will polish _____

3. They were helping _____

4. You all are selling _____

5. She is throwing _____

6. You will shout _____

E. SENTENCE TRANSLATION

Label and translate the following sentences. <u>Underline</u> endings.

1. Iūlia stolam caeruleam et armillam pulchram gestat. ─────────

2. Claudia pallam roseam et ānulum magnum gestat. ─────────

3. Vendītābitne tabernārius Iūliō gladium acūtum? ─────────

4. Saxum scūtum rubrum Claudī līmat. ─────────

5. Puerī citī plaustrum parvum trāns campum movēbant. ─────────

6. Līberī possunt administrāre tabernārium tardum. ─────────

7. Tabernārius Saxō margarītam rotundam mōnstrat. ─────────

F. DERIVATIVES

Choose ten Latin words from Lists 10, 11, and 12 and write them on the blanks on the left. Then give an English derivative for each one.

	LATIN WORD	DERIVATIVE
1.	_____	_____
2.	_____	_____
3.	_____	_____
4.	_____	_____
5.	_____	_____
6.	_____	_____
7.	_____	_____
8.	_____	_____
9.	_____	_____
10.	_____	_____

List Thirteen: Ordinal Numbers

VOCABULARY

Memorize the following words and their translations. Learn the genitive endings for nouns, the second principal parts of verbs, and all three adjective endings.

WORD	DERIVATIVE	TRANSLATION
1. prīmus, -a, -um		*first*
2. secundus, -a, -um		*second*
3. tertius, -a, -um		*third*
4. quartus, -a, -um		*fourth*
5. quintus, -a, -um		*fifth*
6. sextus, -a, -um		*sixth*
7. septimus, -a, um		*seventh*
8. octāvus, -a, -um		*eighth*
9. nōnus, -a, -um		*ninth*
10. decimus, -a, -um		*tenth*
11. argentum, -ī		*silver, money*
12. praemium, -ī		*reward, prize*
13. laurea, -ae		*laurel wreath*
14. adiūdicō, -āre		*award*
15. nūntiō, -āre		*announce*

REVIEW WORDS

1. magister, -trī   *(male) teacher*
2. schola, -ae   *class, classroom*
3. discipulus, -ī   *(boy)student*
4. arithmētica, -ae   *arithmetic*
5. historia, -ae   *history*
6. sella, -ae   *chair, seat*
7. lūdus, -ī   *school, game*
8. magistra, -ae   *female teacher*

FIFTH DECLENSION CHANT

Memorize and copy the new noun chant. It is called Fifth Declension and is the last of the noun families.

FIFTH DECLENSION

-ēs	-ēs
-ēī	-ērum
-ēī	-ēbus
-em	-ēs
-ē	-ēbus

Practice writing the Fifth Declension Chant in the box below:

25 Lesson Twenty-Five: Ordinal Numbers

A. CARDINAL NUMBERS REVIEW

The numbers one to ten are called *cardinal numbers*. They are used to count things. Organize and write the Latin numbers one to ten in order on the blanks below. (Review words from List 8.) *Trēs, decem, octo, quinque, unus, novem, duo, quattuor, septem, sex.*

1. _____
2. _____
3. _____
4. _____
5. _____
6. _____
7. _____
8. _____
9. _____
10. _____

The numbers *unus*, *duo*, and *tres* have masculine, feminine, and neuter endings like other adjectives. However, the endings for *duo* and *tres* are different than regular adjective endings. Study the examples below.

Masculine	Feminine	Neuter
ūnus discipulus *(one boy student)*	ūna discipula *(one girl student)*	ūnum praemium *(one prize)*
duo discipulī *(two boy students)*	duae discipulae *(two girl students)*	duo praemia *(two prizes)*
trēs discipulī *(three boy students)*	trēs discipulae *(three girl students)*	tria praemia *(three prizes)*

N.B. The rest of the cardinal numbers do not change endings!

| septem discipulī *(seven boy students)* | septem discipulae *(seven boy students)* | septem praemia *(seven prizes)* |

B. ORDINAL NUMBERS

Now write the ordinal numbers and their meanings (in order!) from List 13. Ordinal numbers are used to show the order of things. The first one is done for you.

ORDINAL NUMBER   MEANING

1. prīmus, -a, -um   first
2.
3.
4.
5.
6.
7.

Lesson Twenty-Five

8. _____   _____

9. _____   _____

10. _____   _____

N.B. Ordinal numbers are a type of adjective. They have three endings (masculine, feminine, and neuter) just like other adjectives we have learned.

C. PRACTICE

Translate the noun-adjective phrases below. Put them in good English order.

1. discipulus secundus _____

2. magister prīmus _____

3. discipula prīma _____

4. magistra quinta _____

5. praemium decimum _____

D. TRANSLATION

Label and translate the following sentences. Underline endings.

1. Magister Iuliō praemium prīmum in arithmēticā adiūdicat. _____

_____

2. Duo discipulī praemium secundum habent. _____

_____

3. Magister Claudiae lauream in historiā dābit. _____

_____

E. DERIVATIVE DIGGING

Enunciate is an English derivative for the Latin word *nuntiō*. Look up *enunciate* in an English dictionary and write its meaning and write it on the lines below. Then try to use the word *enunciate* in a sentence.

Dictionary definition: _____

_____

Sentence: _____

_____

26 Lesson Twenty-Six: Ordinal Numbers

A. TRANSLATE

Translate these noun-adjective phrases using ordinal numbers into Latin. Put the noun first.

1. first girl _____

2. second school _____

3. ninth boy _____

4. tenth boy student _____

5. eighth prize _____

6. seventh laurel wreath _____

7. fourth chair _____

8. sixth rock _____

9. third class _____

10. fifth male teacher _____

B. CARDINAL NUMBERS REVIEW

Translate these phrases using cardinal numbers. All phrases are in the nominative case. The first one is done as an example:

1. two girls   duae puellae

2. three girls _____

3. three boys _____

4. three rocks _____

5. one toga _____

6. two shoes _____

7. two prizes _____

8. five shields _____

9. ten jewels _____

10. seven rings _____

C. TRANSLATE

Label and translate these sentences. <u>Underline</u> endings. Be on the look out for these parts of speech: SN, DO, IO, PNA, OP, V, V-t, P, ADJ. Both ordinal and cardinal numbers are used.

1. Ūnus magister adiūdicābat. _____

_____

2. Duo magistrī praemium tertium adiūdicābant. _____

_____

3. Trēs magistrae quattuor puellīs quīnque laureās adiūdicābant. _____

_____

4. Magister ludī Iūliō praemium quintum adiūdicābant. _____

_____

5. Discipula prīma Iūliae argentum in scholā dat. _____

_____

6. Decem magistrī Saxō lauream prīmam dat. _____

_____

D. TIDBIT

The laurel wreath (made of leaves from the laurel tree) was a symbol of victory for both the Greeks and Romans. Beyond military victories, people who were very respected in the arts, government, and education might also wear laurel wreaths. Laurel wreaths worn by kings were decorated with gold and jewels which later became crowns.

14 List Fourteen: Exploring a Cave

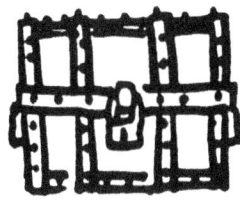

A. VOCABULARY

Memorize the following Latin words and their translations. Learn the genitive forms for nouns, the second principal parts for verbs, and all three endings for adjectives.

WORD	DERIVATIVE	TRANSLATION
1. ferus, -ī		*wild animal*
2. spēlunca, -ae		*cave*
3. thēsaurus, -ī		*treasure*
4. accūrātus,-a,-um		*careful, exact*
5. timidus,-a,-um		*fearful*
6. animōsus, -a,-um		*courageous*
7. hodiē		*today*
8. heri		*yesterday*
9. crās		*tomorrow*
10. vocō, -āre		*call*
11. astō, -āre		*stand near*
12. exspectō, -āre		*wait for*
13. retineō, -ēre		*hold back*
14. fugitō, -āre		*flee from*
15. explorō, -āre		*explore*

REVIEW WORDS

1. magnus, -a, -um — *large*
2. īrātus, -a, -um — *angry*
3. tardus, -a, -um — *slow*
4. citus, -a, -um — *fast, swift*
5. latus, -a, -um — *wide*
6. mannulus, -ī — *pony*
7. ululō, -āre — *howl, scream*
8. gemma, -ae — *jewel*
9. aurum, -ī — *gold*
10. armilla, -ae — *bracelet*
11. anulus, -ī — *ring*
12. margarīta, -ae — *pearl*
13. praemium, -ī — *reward, prize*

List Fourteen

27 Lesson Twenty-Seven: Exploring a Cave

A. ADVERBS

An adverb describes a verb, adjective, or another adverb. It can tell *how, when,* or *where*. In English, we can often create an adverb by adding the ending **-ly** to an adjective. Compare some adjectives and their adverb forms:

ADJECTIVE	ADVERB
1. careful	carefully
2. fearful	fearfully
3. courageous	courageously

In Latin, we can also turn an adjective into an adverb by adding a different ending. Here is the rule for creating Latin adverbs:

Remove the feminine ending from a Latin adjective in order to find the base of the adjective. Then add the adverb ending -ē to the base.

LATIN ADJECTIVE (feminine form)	BASE	LATIN ADVERB	TRANSLATION
1. accurata	accurat-	accuratē	carefully
2. timida	timid-	timidē	fearfully
3. animosa	animos-	animosē	courageously

N.B. It is important to use the feminine form of a Latin adjective when making an adverb because sometimes there is a spelling change between the masculine and feminine forms. Consider the example of the adjective which means beautiful, handsome:

M.	F.	N.	ADVERB
pulcher	*pulchra*	*pulchrum*	*pulchrē* (not *pulche*)

Other adverbs are not created from an adjective. For example, on our list we have the adverbs *hodiē* (today), *heri* (yesterday), and *crās* (tomorrow).

N.B. ADVERBS DO NOT CHANGE THEIR ENDINGS!

B. PRACTICE

Translate these adverbs created from adjectives we have studied before:

1. magnē _____

2. acutē _____

3. īrātē _____

4. tardē _____

5. lātē _____

6. citē _____

C. TRANSLATE

Label and translate the following sentences. <u>Underline</u> endings on nouns, verbs, adjectives, and adverbs!

1. Līberī spēluncam magnam animōsē explorant. _____

2. Iūlius thēsaurum pulchrum videt et Claudium vocat. _____

3. Iūlius et Claudius thēsaurum astant. _____

4. Iūlia ferum magnum videt et ululat! _____

5. Līberī ferum fugitant citē. _____

6. Claudia animosa ferum timidum exspectat. _____

7. Ferus magnus est* mannulus parvus! _____

*est = is

Lesson Twenty-Seven

28 Lesson Twenty-Eight: Exploring a Cave

A. DATIVE CASE REVIEW

Circle the correct part of speech represented by the dative case.

    subject noun   direct object   possessive noun   indirect object

Now give the dative forms of the words below:

	DATIVE SINGULAR	DATIVE PLURAL
1. ferus		
2. magistra		
3. saxum		

B. ADVERB REVIEW

Adverbs are formed by removing the _____ ending from an adjective and adding -ē.

Adverbs can tell what three things?

_____ , _____ , and _____ .

Make these adjectives into adverbs and then translate the adverbs.

ADJECTIVE	ADVERB	ADVERB TRANSLATION
1. accūrātus		
2. timidus		

3. animōsus _____   _____

4. acūtus _____   _____

5. pulcher _____   _____

C. TRANSLATE

Label and translate the following sentences. <u>Underline</u> endings. Labels to choose from: SN, V, V-t, DO, IO, PNA, P, OP, ADJ, ADV. Sentence #3 also contains a command or imperative (labeled IMP).

1. Iūlia et mannulus fulvus ambulābant tardē in speluncā. _____

2. Iūlius, Claudius, et Claudia properābant trans campum ad speluncam. _____

3. Claudia vocābat: "Iulia, exspectā." _____

4. Claudia Iūliam et manulum fulvum astābat. _____

5. Iūlius et Claudius thēsaurum magnum spectābant. _____

6. Līberī armillās caeruleās, aurum flavum, gemmās rubrās, anulōs nigrōs, et margaritās albās portābant accurātē. _____

7. Mannulus parvus administrābat portāre aurum. _____

8. Līberī mannulō parvō praemium dābant. _____

Lesson Twenty-Eight

15 List Fifteen: Adventure at the River

VOCABULARY

Memorize the following Latin words and their translations. Learn the genitive forms for nouns, the second principal parts for verbs, and all three endings for the adjective.

WORD	DERIVATIVE	TRANSLATION
1. rīpa, -ae	_____	*riverbank*
2. fluvius, -ī	_____	*river*
3. lignum, -ī	_____	*log*
4. muscōsus, -a, -um	_____	*mossy*
5. saepe	_____	*often*
6. semper	_____	*always*
7. repentē	_____	*suddenly*
8. bene	_____	*well*
9. nunc	_____	*now*
10. tum	_____	*then*
11. diū	_____	*for a long time*
12. firmō, -āre	_____	*strengthen*
13. nō, -āre	_____	*swim*
14. redundō, -āre	_____	*overflow*
15. servo, -āre	_____	*save*

List Fifteen

REVIEW WORDS

1. mūrus, -ī   wall, dike
2. trans   across
3. in (w/abl.)   in, on
4. erro, -āre   wander
5. sedeō, -ēre   sit
6. fugitō, -āre   flee
7. sed   but

List Fifteen

29 Lesson Twenty-Nine: Adventure at the River

A. ADVERB REVIEW

Definition of an adverb: An adverb modifies a verb, _____, or another _____.

An adverb tells how, _____, or where.

To create an adverb in English, we can often add the ending _____ to an adjective.

To form an adverb in Latin, remove the _____ ending from the Latin adjective and add _____ .

Translate these adverbs into English:

1. timidē _____

2. animōsē _____

3. pulchrē _____

4. accūratē _____

5. tardē _____

Other adverbs are not formed from adjectives. Write the other seven adverbs from List 15 on the lines below: (one adverb is given)

tum,_____
_____

B. TRANSLATE

Label and translate the following sentences. Underline endings on nouns, verbs, and adjectives.

N.B. The imperfect tense endings (*bam, bās, bat, bāmus, bātis, bant*) can sometimes be translated with *used to* instead of *was/were*.

1. Līberī et Saxum saepe errābant in rīpā. _____

2. Nunc Iūlius et Claudius ambulant trans fluvium in mūrō. _____

3. Iūlia, Claudia, et Saxum diū sedebant in lignō muscōsō. _____

4. Repente fluvius redundābat! _____

5. Iūlius nat bene sed Claudius nōn nat bene. _____

6. Tum Iūlius Claudium servat. _____

7. Iūlia, Claudia, et Saxum iuvābant citē. _____

8. Līberī et Saxum mūrum bene firmant. _____

C. VERB PRACTICE

Underline endings and translate the following verbs:

1. redundābunt _____

2. servāmus _____

Lesson Twenty-Nine

3. nabātis   _____

4. firmābō   _____

5. redundābās _____

6. servābat   _____

D. TIDBIT

Rome is located on the river Tiber, the third longest river in Italy.

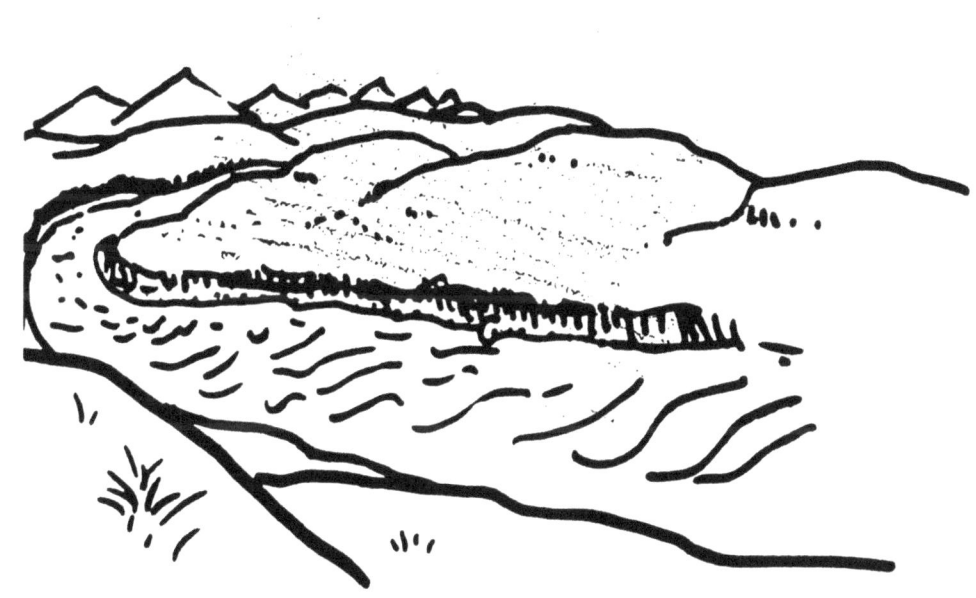

30 Lesson Thirty: Adventure at the River

A. REVIEW CARDINAL NUMBERS

Use cardinal numbers to translate the following phrases into English. Only numbers *one, two,* and *three* must match the nouns they describe in gender, number, and case. The higher numbers do not change. All are in the nominative case.

1. tria saxa   _____
2. trēs laureae   _____
3. septem puerī   _____
4. ūnum lignum   _____
5. duo ferī   _____
6. duae spēluncae   _____
7. ūnus thēsaurus   _____
8. ūna rīpa   _____
9. octō fluviī   _____
10. decem ligna   _____

B. REVIEW ORDINAL NUMBERS

Translate these phrases using ordinal numbers. All are in the nominative case.

1. laurea tertia   _____
2. fluvius septimus   _____

3. lignum decimum _____

4. thēsaurus prīmus _____

5. rīpa quarta _____

C. TRANSLATE

Translate these adverbs into Latin.

1. carefully _____

2. courageously _____

3. fearfully _____

4. beautifully _____

5. gratefully _____

D. MACARONIC STORY

A macaronic story mixes words from two languages. Write a short story in English, using at east five adjectives and five adverbs from Lists 13, 14, and 15. Underline the Latin adjectives and adverbs you use.

_____
_____
_____
_____
_____
_____
_____

Unit Five Review

A. VOCABULARY

From memory, translate as many of these vocabulary words as you can. Then look up any you don't remember.

1. tertius, -a, -um _____

2. thēsaurus, -ī _____

3. muscōsus, -a, -um _____

4. semper _____

5. crās _____

6. argentum, -ī _____

7. nuntiō, -āre _____

8. animōsus, -a, -um _____

9. nunc _____

10. redundō, -āre _____

11. retineō, -ēre _____

12. septimus, -a, -um _____

13. fugitō, -āre _____

14. lignum, -ī _____

15. bene _____

English to Latin:

16. wait for _____

17. reward, prize _____

18. swim _____

19. award (verb) _____

20. cave _____

B. CHANT REVIEW

Fill in the following chant:

FIFTH DECLENSION

-ēs	
-ēī	

C. CARDINAL NUMBERS

The cardinal numbers *unus, duo,* and *tres* act like other Latin adjectives because they must match the nouns they describe in gender, number, and case. Translate these noun-adjective phrases. All are in the nominative case and the first one is done as an example.

1. one riverbank   ūna rīpa

2. three laurel wreaths   _____

3. two rivers   _____

4. one treasure   _____

5. two caves _____

6. one reward _____

7. three logs _____

D. ORDINAL NUMBERS

Ordinal numbers must also match the nouns they describe in gender, number, and case. Translate these noun-adjective phrases. All are in the nominative case and the first one is done as an example.

1. the first silver   argentum primun

2. the second classroom _____

3. the third male teacher _____

4. the fourth wild animal _____

5. the fifth seat _____

6. the sixth school _____

7. the seventh pony _____

8. the eighth pearl _____

9. the ninth log _____

10. the tenth wall _____

E. ADVERB TRANSLATION

Translate these adverbs. Remember, adverbs are formed by removing the feminine ending and adding the adverb ending -e.

1. timidē _____

2. animōsē _____

3. accūrātē _____

English to Latin:

1. angrily   ———————————————

2. swiftly   ———————————————

3. widely   ———————————————

F. SENTENCE TRANSLATION

Label and translate the following sentences. <u>Underline endings.</u>

1. Magister īrātus discipulum prīmum vocābat īrātē. ———————————————

2. Puella timida errābat in rīpā timidē. ———————————————

3. Saxum nōn bene potest nāre trans fluvium lātum. ———————————————

4. Fluvius citus rīpam lātam diū redundābit. ———————————————

5. Nunc magistra praemium prīmum nuntiat. ———————————————

6. Iūlia accurātē ambulat trans lignum muscōsum. ———————————————

G. DERIVATIVES

Choose three derivatives from Lists 13, 14, or 15 and tell their Latin origins. Look up each word in an English dictionary and write the definition on the lines provided. Then use one of your derivatives in a sentence.

1. Word _____

    Latin Origin _____

    Definition _____

    _____

2. Word _____

    Latin Origin _____

    Definition _____

    _____

3. Word _____

    Latin Origin _____

    Definition _____

    _____

    Sentence: _____

    _____

Unit 5 Review 181

16 List Sixteen: Robbers!

VOCABULARY

Memorize the following Latin words and their translations. In addition to knowing the genitive forms of nouns, also learn the gender (masculine, feminine, or neuter). Also know the second principal parts of the verbs.

Word	Derivative	Translation
1. pārens, parentis, *m.* or *f.*	_____	*parent*
2. canis, canis, *m.* or *f.**	_____	*dog*
3. fēles, fēlis, *f.*	_____	*cat*
4. psittacus, -ī *m.*	_____	*parrot*
5. praedo, praedōnis, *m.*	_____	*robber*
6. frutex, fruticis, *m.*	_____	*bush*
7. lex, lēgis, *f.*	_____	*law*
8. nox, noctis, *f.*	_____	*night*
9. pāreō, -ēre	_____	*obey*
10. inlaqueō, -āre	_____	*entrap*
11. comportō, -āre	_____	*collect*
12. sībilō, -āre	_____	*whistle, hiss* (at)
13. lātrō, -āre	_____	*bark* (at)
14. exspolio, -āre	_____	*rob*
15. a, ab	_____	*from, away from* (prep. w/abl.)

*Canis is an exception to the rule; it is not a Third Declension I-Stem.

List Sixteen   183

REVIEW WORDS

1. frater, fratris, *m.* — *brother*
2. soror, sorōris, *f.* — *sister*
3. pater, patris, *m.* — *father*
4. mater, matris, *f.* — *mother*
5. pecunia, -ae, *f.* — *money*
6. argentum, -ī, *n.* — *silver, money*
7. aurum, -ī, *n.* — *gold*
8. gemma, -ae, *f.* — *jewel*
9. sedeō, -ēre — *sit*
10. in (w/abl.) — *in or on*
11. lectus, -ī, *m.* — *bed*
12. cubō, -āre — *lie down*
13. ululō, -āre — *howl, scream*
14. domus, -ūs, *f.** — *home, house*
15. occultō, -āre — *hide*

*This word is from the fourth declension but has some second declension characteristics.

31 Lesson Thirty-One: Robbers!

A. NOUN CHANT REVIEW

Fill in the noun chants below:

FIRST DECLENSION

-a	
-ae	

SECOND DECLENSION

-us	
-ī	

SECOND DECLENSION NEUTER

-um	
-ī	

THIRD DECLENSION

-x	
-is	

Highlight the genitive singular ending for each declension in the boxes.

When the genitive singular ending is **-is**, then the noun is in **third declension**. The third declension nominative ending **-x** represents many different endings. Identify third declension nouns by looking at the genitive endings on List 16 and highlight nouns from the third declension.

What are some third declension nominative singular endings in addition to **-x**? Write those endings on the line below.

Third declension nominative singular endings: _____

B. THIRD DECLENSION

In the first box below, the third declension noun *lex, legis* is declined for you. Study it carefully, then decline (put endings on) the third declension noun *praedo, praedonis*. Find the base of the noun first by removing the genitive ending.

N.B. Don't try to change the case until you find the base. The genitive case is the place to find the base!

lex	legēs
legis	legum
legī	legibus
legem	legēs
lege	legibus

praedo	
praedonis	

Lesson Thirty-One

C. TRANSLATION

<u>Underline</u> endings on nouns and verbs. Highlight any third declension nouns, then label and translate these Pattern 1 sentences.

1. Praedō exspoliābat. _____

2. Canis latrat. _____

3. Fēles sībilat. _____

4. Psittacus ululābat. _____

5. Parentēs occultant. _____

6. Iūlius et Iūlia inlaqueant. _____

7. Saxum sedēbit. _____

Challenge: Translate these two sentences. How can you tell which one is singular and which one is plural?

Fēles sībilat. _____

Fēlēs sībilant. _____

D. TIDBIT

The Romans used dogs much as we do. They were pets, farm dogs, or watch dogs. An ancient sign was unearthed which said "*Cave Canem.*" Can you guess what that might mean?

_____

Lesson Thirty-One

32 Lesson Thirty-Two: Robbers!

A. PRACTICE

To find the base of a noun, remove the _____ ending from the noun.

Practice declining more third declension nouns below. Remember to find the base first.

frutex	
fruticis	

lex	
lēgis	

B. COMPARISON

Compare the Third Declension Chant with its cousin, Third Declension I-stem Chant.

Circle the ending (other than the nominative singular) which is different in the third I-stem chart below. Now highlight the accusative endings in both the third declension and the third I-stem Chants.

THIRD DECLENSION

-x	-ēs
-is	-um
-ī	-ibus
-em	-ēs
-e	-ibus

THIRD DECLENSION I-STEM

-is	-ēs
-is	-ium
-ī	-ibus
-em	-ēs
-e	-ibus

Decline this third declension noun in the box below.

canis*	
canis	

N.B. Other third declension i-stem nouns on List 16 are: *pārēns, fēles,* and *nox.*

*Canis is not an i-stem noun; it is an exception to the rule.

C. TRANSLATION

Underline endings, label, and translate these sentences. Most are Pattern 2. Highlight any adjectives.

1. Praedōnēs dōmum exspoliābant. _____

2. Canis praedōnem prīmum lātrat. _____

3. Felēs praedōnem secundum sībilat. _____

4. Parentēs pecūniam et aurum occultant. _____

5. Iūlius et Iūlia praedōnem prīmum inlaqueant. _____

6. Saxum sedet in praedōne secundō! _____

N.B. Notice that the adjectives you highlighted match these 3rd declension nouns in gender, number and case, but not in declension.

D. DERIVATIVE DIGGING

When do *nocturnal* animals hunt for food? _____

List Seventeen: Courtroom

VOCABULARY

Memorize the following Latin words and their translations. Know genitive forms and genders for nouns and the second principal parts of verbs.

Word	Derivative	Translation
1. iūdex, iūdicis, *m.*		*judge, juror*
2. mīles, mīlitis, *m.*		*soldier*
3. testis, testis, *m.* or *f.*		*witness*
4. testimōnium, -ī, *n.*		*testimony*
5. carcer, carceris, *m.*		*prison*
6. sententia, -ae, *f.*		*opinion, decision*
7. cīvis, cīvis, m. or *f.*		*citizen*
8. praefectus, -ī, *m.*		*officer, official*
9. iūdicium, -ī, *n.*		*trial, court of law*
10. vigilō, -āre		*guard*
11. damnō, -āre		*condemn*
12. imperō, -āre		*order*
13. relēgō, -āre		*send away*
14. avārus, -a, -um		*greedy*
15. scelerātus, -a, -um		*guilty*

REVIEW WORDS

1. praedō, praedōnis, m. — *robber*
2. stō, stāre — *stand*
3. tardus,-a,-um — *slow*
4. duo — *two*
5. moneō, -ēre — *warn*
6. calcitrō, -āre — *kick*
7. nuntiō, -āre — *announce*
8. astō, astare — *stand near*
9. narrō, -āre — *tell*
10. dō, -āre — *give*
11. vocō, -āre — *call*

VERB REVIEW

Fill in the meanings of the verb endings below:

PRESENT TENSE

-ō -	-mus -
-s -	-tis -
-t -	-nt -

IMPERFECT TENSE

-bam -	-bāmus -
-bās -	-bātis -
-bat -	-bant -

FUTURE TENSE

-bō -	-bimus -
-bis -	-bitis -
-bit -	-bunt -

List Seventeen

33 Lesson Thirty-Three: Courtroom

A. PARTS OF SPEECH

Below are words from List 17. Each one has a related word on List 17. Find the related word, then label each one according to its part of speech. Look for similar spellings and similar meanings.

	Related Word	Part of Speech
iudex, iudicis	_____	_____
testis, testis	_____	_____

B. CONJUGATE AND TRANSLATE

Conjugate and translate *damnō* in the present tense:

damnō - *I condemn*	

Conjugate and translate *imperō* in the imperfect tense:

imperābam - *I was ordering*	

Conjugate and translate *rēlegō* in the future tense:

relegābō - *I will send away*	

C. TRANSLATION

Study the correct and *incorrect* versions of the sentence below. Then label and translate these Pattern 1 (SN-V) sentences into Latin. Be sure to put the correct endings on the verbs.

What case do subject nouns go in? _____

Example: The citizen shouts.

   Incorrect (Can you tell what is wrong?)

   Cīvis clāmō.
   Cīvis clāmābat.
   Cīvēs clāmat.

   Correct

   Cīvis clāmat.

Translate:

1. The officer announces. _____

2. The officers order. _____

3. The soldier stands near. _____

4. The soldiers were standing near. _____

5. The judge sends away. _____

Now label and translate these Pattern 2 (SN V-t DO) sentences into Latin.

What case do direct objects go in? _____

1. The officer announces the trial. _____

2. The soldiers were standing near the citizen. _____

_____

3. The witnesses will give testimony. _____

_____

4. The judge sends away the robbers. _____

_____

D. DERIVATIVE DIGGING

Look up the English word *sentence* in the dictionary and read the defintions for the word. On the lines below, write the definition of *sentence* which most closely matches the meaning of the Latin word *sententia*.

sentence- _____

_____

Lesson Thirty-Three

34 Lesson Thirty-Four: Courtroom

A. GENITIVE REVIEW

Give the genitive forms of these nouns.

NOUN	GENITIVE SINGULAR	GENITIVE PLURAL
1. iūdex		
2. testis		
3. carcer		
4. testimōnium		
5. sententia		
6. praefectus		

What part of speech is the genitive case used for? _____

B. ACCUSATIVE REVIEW

Give the accusative forms of the following nouns:

NOUN	ACCUSATIVE SINGULAR	ACCUSATIVE PLURAL
1. iūdex		
2. testis		
3. carcer		
4. testimōnium		

5. sententia _____   _____

6. praefectus _____   _____

What part of speech is the accusative case used for? _____

C. TRANSLATE

Label and translate the following sentences. <u>Underline</u> endings on nouns and verbs.

1. Cīvēs sedēbant in iudiciō. _____
   _____

2. Praefectus cīvēs imperat, "Stāte." _____

3. Mīlites praedōnēs astābant et vigilābant. _____
   _____

4. Iūdex testem vocat. _____

5. Iūlius, Iūlia, et parentēs testimōnium dant. _____
   _____

6. Damnābitne iūdex praedōnēs avārōs? _____
   _____

7. Iūdex praedōnēs scelerātōs relēgat ad carcerem. _____
   _____

C. TIDBIT

Romans did not use time in prison as punishment. Usually Roman prisons held only those condemned to die for their crimes. Rich people awaiting trial might be under house arrest until their case was tried or went to court. The Apostle Paul was able to be under house arrest when he was in Rome.

18 List Eighteen: Government

VOCABULARY

Memorize the following Latin words and their translations. Know genitive forms and genders for nouns and the second principal parts of verbs.

Word	Derivative	Translation
1. senātor, senātōris, *m.*	_____	*senator*
2. cōnsul, cōnsulis, *m.*	_____	*consul*
3. iānitor, iānitōris, *m.*	_____	*doorkeeper*
4. avunculus, -ī, *m.*	_____	*uncle*
5. filius sorōris	_____	*nephew*
6. filia sorōris	_____	*niece*
7. basilica, -ae, *f.*	_____	*court building*
8. cūria, -ae, *f.*	_____	*senate building*
9. limbus, -ī, *m.*	_____	*border, hem*
10. iānua, -ae, *f.*	_____	*door*
11. purpureus, -a, -um	_____	*purple*
12. intrō, -āre	_____	*enter*
13. disputō, -āre	_____	*discuss, argue*
14. gubernō, -āre	_____	*govern, steer*
15. creō, -āre	_____	*make, create*

REVIEW WORDS

1. forum, -ī, *n.* — *public square*
2. toga, -ae, *f.* — *toga*
3. Rōma, -ae, *f.* — *Rome*
4. iūdex, iūdicis, *m.* — *judge*
5. vīsitō, -āre — *visit*
6. gestō, -āre — *wear*
7. praedo, praedōnis, *m.* — *robber*
8. pareō, -ēre — *obey*
9. lex, lēgis, *f.* — *law*
10. est — *is*
11. vigilō, -āre — *guard*
12. ā, ab — *from, away from* (prep. w/abl.)
13. ad — *to, toward* (prep. w/acc.)
14. quod — *because*
15. bonus, -a, um — *good*
16. senex*, senis, *m.* — *old man*

*This word has not been previously introduced, but will be used on p.210. It is also listed in the glossary.

List Eighteen

35 Lesson Thirty-Five: Government

A. CHANT REVIEW

From memory, try to complete the noun declension chants and examples of each declension below. <u>Underline</u> all nominative endings in blue and all accusative endings in red.

FIRST DECLENSION

-a	
-ae	

cūria	
cūriae	

SECOND DECLENSION

-us	
-ī	

avunculus	
avunculī	

SECOND DECLENSION NEUTER

-um	
-ī	

forum	
forī	

THIRD DECLENSION

-x	
-is	

lex	
lēgis	

Lesson Thirty-Five

B. BASE OF A NOUN

Can you fill in the missing parts of the jingle below about finding the base of a noun?

Don't try to change the _____

until you find the _____ .

The _____ case

is the _____

to find the _____ .

Give the genitive singular and base for each of the nouns below:

NOMINATIVE	GENITIVE	BASE
1. cūria		
2. avunculus		
3. forum		
4. lex		

C. VERB PRACTICE

Conjugate and translate the verbs below. Circle the correct conjugation.

PRESENT TENSE Is *creo, -āre* first conjugation ("A" Family) or second conjugation ("E" Family)?

creō -	

IMPERFECT TENSE Is *guberno, -āre* first conjugation ("A" Family) or second conjugation ("E" Family)?

gubernābam -	

FUTURE TENSE Is *pareo, -ēre* first conjugation ("A" Family) or second conjugation ("E" Family)?

parēbō -	

D. TRANSLATE

Label and translate these Pattern 1 sentences into Latin. The first one is done as an example.

    SN   V
1. The consul governs. Cōnsul gubernat. _____

2. The doorkeeper was guarding. _____

3. The senators will discuss. _____

4. The nephew and niece were obeying. _____

E. CHALLENGE QUESTION

Why do the Latin phrases *filius sororis* and *filia sorōris* make sense for our English words *nephew* and *niece*?

_____

_____

_____

_____

Lesson Thirty-Five 207

36 Lesson Thirty-Six: Government

A. DECLENSION PRACTICE

Identify the declensions (1st, 2nd, 2nd N. or 3rd) of the nouns below by looking at their genitive singular endings:

NOUN	DECLENSION
1. senātor, senātōris	_____
2. basilica, -ae	_____
3. forum, -ī	_____
4. iūdex, iūdicis	_____
5. avunculus, -ī	_____
6. limbus, -ī	_____

B. ADJECTIVE REVIEW

Adjectives must match the nouns they describe in what three ways?

1. _____

2. _____

3. _____

Adjectives do not always match in declension. For example, the word *senex* is masculine, singular, and nominative. Therefore the adjective which describes it must be masculine, singular, and nominative. Study the example below:

	CORRECT	INCORRECT
(Masculine example) *the greedy old man*	senex avarus	senex avarex
(Feminine example) *the first law*	lex prīma	lex prīmex

C. TRANSLATE

Translate these noun-adjective phrases in the nominative case. Remember, adjectives match nouns in gender, number, and case, but not always declension!

1. cōnsul scelerātus _____

2. iānitōr rotundus _____

3. avunculus acūtus _____

4. māter bona _____

5. curia magna _____

6. limbus purpureus _____

D. TRANSLATE

Underline endings, label, and translate the sentences below:

1. Iūlius, Iūlia, et parentēs ambulant ā basilicā ad curiam. _____

2. Visitābunt avunculum līberōrum. _____

Lesson Thirty-Six

3. Iūlius est filius sorōris avunculī et Iūlia est filia sorōris avunculī. _____

4. Avunculus gestat limbum purpureum in togā quod est senātor. _____

5. Avunculus et senātōrēs lēgēs bonās creant. _____

6. Duo consulēs Rōmam gubernant. _____

7. Iānitōr magnus curiam astat et iānuam vigilat. _____

8. Senātōrēs lēgēs disputant et līberī et parentēs auscultant. _____

E. TIDBIT

In the Roman republic two consuls were appointed to rule together. The office of the consul was the highest governmental office. Consuls served a term of only one year. Each consul could veto (cancel out) a decision of the other consul.

Unit Six Review

A. VOCABULARY

From memory, translate as many of these vocabulary words as you can. Then look up any you don't remember.

1. ā, ab _____

2. psittacus, -ī _____

3. exspoliō, -āre _____

4. fīlius sorōris _____

5. nox, noctis _____

6. limbus, -ī _____

7. frutex, fruticis _____

8. iūdex, iūdicis _____

9. avunculus, -ī _____

10. vigilō, -āre _____

11. avārus, -a, -um _____

12. carcer, carceris _____

13. sententia, -ae _____

14. mīles, mīlitis _____

15. senātor, senātōris _____

English to Latin

16. law _____

17. testimony _____

18. purple _____

19. whistle, hiss (at) _____

20. citizen _____

B. CHANTS

Fill in these noun chants:

THIRD DECLENSION

-x	
-is	

THIRD DECLENSION I-STEM

-is	
-is	

C. FILL IN THE BLANKS

Fill in the blanks about gender. Choose from masculine, feminine, or neuter.

1. Most first declension ("A" Family) nouns are _____ .

2. Most second declension ("Us" Family) nouns are _____ .

3. Second declension neuter nouns are _____ .

Now write the gender (masculine, feminine, or neuter) of these third declension nouns.

4. iūdex, iūdicis _____

5. testis, testis _____

6. praedō, praedōnis _____

7. lex, lēgis _____

8. canis, canis _____

9. iānitor, iānitōris _____

10. fēles, fēlis _____

D. ADJECTIVE MATCHING

Circle the correct form of the adjective to match the nouns below. Remember, adjectives match nouns in gender, number, and case, but not always in declension. Some nouns can be masculine or feminine. In that case, circle both.

NOUN	ADJECTIVE		
	(Masculine)	(Feminine)	(Neuter)
1. psittacus	purpureus	purpurea	purpureum
2. praedō	scelerātus	scelerāta	scelerātum
3. nox	primus	prima	primum
4. canis	bonus	bona	bonum
5. fēles	malus	mala	malum

E. TRANSLATION

Translate these verbs. Underline endings.

1. sībilant _____

2. latrābit _____

3. parēbimus _____

4. inlaqueābās _____

5. comportābō _____

6. disputatis _____

7. relegābat _____

8. creābunt _____

F. SENTENCE TRANSLATION

Label and translate these sentences. Underline endings.

1. Canēs praedōnem latrābant in fruticē. _____

_____

2. Testis prīmus testimōnium dat in iūdiciō. _____

_____

3. Praedō avārus lēgem non parēbat. _____

_____

4. Consul praedōnēs scelerātōs relegābit ad carcerem. _____

_____

5. Cīvēs lēgem parēbunt. _____

_____

G. DERIVATIVE PRACTICE

Look over Lists 16, 17, and 18. Choose two derivatives from each list (six derivatives total) and write them on the lines provided. On the other lines, write the Latin origin for each derivative.

DERIVATIVE   LATIN ORIGIN

1. _____   _____

2. _____   _____

3. _____   _____

4. _____   _____

5. _____   _____

6. _____   _____

Challenge: Use one of your derivatives in a good English sentence.

_____

_____

Unit 6 Review   217

19 List Nineteen: Insects and Reptiles

VOCABULARY

Memorize the following Latin words and their translations. Know genitive forms and genders for nouns and the second principal parts of verbs.

Word	Derivative	Translation
1. bēstiola, -ae, *f.*	_____	*insect*
2. bēstia serpēns, *f.*	_____	*reptile*
3. cicāda, -ae, *f.*	_____	*tree cricket*
4. gryllus, -ī, *m.*	_____	*grasshopper*
5. arānea, -ae, *f.*	_____	*spider*
6. tēla, -ae, *f.*	_____	*web*
7. serpēns, serpentis, *m.* or *f.*	_____	*snake*
8. lacerta, -ae, *f.*	_____	*lizard*
9. grāmen, grāminis, *n.*	_____	*grass*
10. crūs, crūris, *n.*	_____	*leg*
11. neō, -ēre	_____	*spin, weave*
12. provolō, -āre	_____	*dart, dash*
13. mandūcō, -āre	_____	*chew, eat*
14. tītillō, -āre	_____	*tickle*
15. inter	_____	*between, among* (prep. w/ acc.)

List Nineteen

REVIEW WORDS

1. folium, -ī, *n.* — *leaf*
2. inlaqueō, -āre — *entrap*
3. occultō, -āre — *hide*
4. cantō, -āre — *sing*
5. sībilō, -āre — *whistle at, hiss at*
6. arbor, arboris, *f.* — *tree*
7. saxum, saxī, *n.* — *rock*
8. habeō, -ēre — *have, hold*

THIRD DECLENSION NEUTER CHANT

Memorize Third Declension Neuter Chant. It is a cousin of Third Declension.

THIRD DECLENSION NEUTER

-x	-a
-is	-um
-ī	-ibus
-x	-a
-e	-ibus

Practice writing the Third Declension Neuter Chant in the box below:

THIRD DECLENSION NEUTER

N.B. Neuter nouns always look the same in the nominative and accusative cases. Also, the nominative and accusative plural endings are always **-a**.

37 Lesson Thirty-Seven: Insects and Reptiles

A. THIRD DECLENSION NEUTER

Compare the regular Third Declension Noun Chant with the Third Declension Neuter. Highlight or circle the places where the Third Declension Neuter is different.

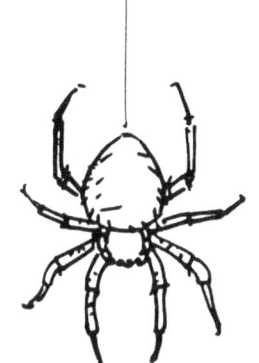

THIRD DECLENSION

-x	-ēs
-is	-um
-ī	-ibus
-em	-ēs
-e	-ibus

THIRD DECLENSION NEUTER

-x	-a
-is	-um
-ī	-ibus
-x	-a
-e	-ibus

Study the example of a third declension neuter noun as it is declined below.

N.B. *Crus, cruris* might look like a second declension noun at first glance. This is why you always need to look at the genitive ending!

Highlight or circle the nominative and accusative forms.

Nom.	crūs	crūra
Gen.	crūris	crūrum
Dat.	crūrī	crūribus
Acc.	crūs	crūra
Abl.	crūre	crūribus

What do you notice about the nominative and accusative forms? _____

_____

Lesson Thirty-Seven 221

Decline the third declension neuter noun below. Be sure to find the base of the noun first!

Nom.	grāmen	
Gen.	grāminis	
Dat.		
Acc.		
Abl.		

B. VERB REVIEW

We have learned two verb families, the "A" Family and the "E" Family. Officially, we refer to verb families as *conjugations*. Fill in the blanks about conjugations below.

The first conjugation is known as the _____ Family because it has the letter _____ before its endings.

The second conjugation is known as the _____ Family because it has the letter _____ before its endings.

Give an example of a first conjugation verb from List 19. _____

Translate these verbs:

1. tītillābāmus   _____

2. provolātis   _____

3. nēbō   _____

4. mandūcābunt   _____

5. tītillābās   _____

6. nēbitis   _____

C. TRANSLATION

Consider these Pattern 2 sentences. At first glance, they may not seem like Pattern 2 sentences because no subject noun is named. A subject *pronoun* is present — it is just hiding in the verb ending! <u>Underline</u> endings, label, and translate the sentences below. The first one is done as an example.

    V-t   DO
1. Nē<u>bat</u> tēl<u>am</u>.   He, she, it was spinning a web.

2. Mandūcat grāmen. _____

3. Tītillābunt lacertās. _____

4. Inlaqueābis bēstiolam. _____

5. Occultābō gryllum. _____

Challenge Sentence: Serpentēs non sībilāmus. _____

Challenge Question: Why do you have to be careful with the noun *crūs, crūris*? _____

Lesson Thirty-Seven

38 Lesson Thirty-Eight: Insects and Reptiles

A. NOMINATIVE AND ACCUSATIVE REVIEW

Highlight the nominative and accusative endings in the charts below:

SECOND DECLENSION NEUTER

Nom.	-um	-a
Gen.	-ī	-ōrum
Dat.	-ō	-īs
Acc.	-um	-a
Abl.	-ō	-īs

THIRD DECLENSION NEUTER

Nom.	-x	-a
Gen.	-is	-um
Dat.	-ī	-ibus
Acc.	-x	-a
Abl.	-e	-ibus

Fill in the blanks.

Neuter nouns always look the _____ in the nominative and accusative cases!

Neuter nouns always end in _____ in the nominative and accusative plural.

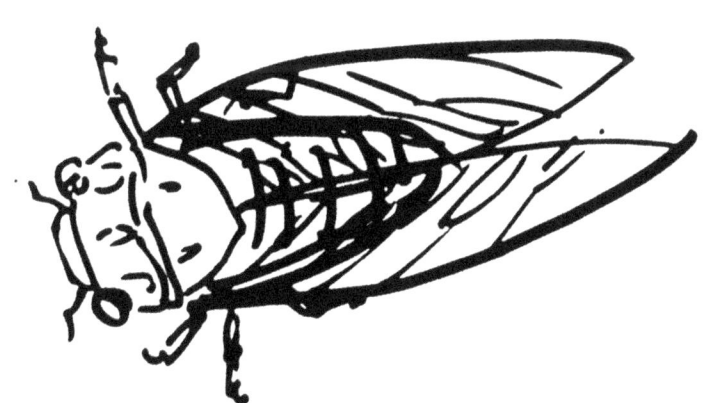

B. MORE ABOUT NEUTER NOUNS

Because neuter nouns look the same in the nominative and accusative cases, it is necessary to be more careful when identifying whether the neuter noun is a subject or a direct object. Examine this sentence which contains both of the third declension neuter nouns from List 19.

    Grāmen crūs tītillat.

Notice that both *grāmen* and *crūs* are third declension neuter nouns. Both could be either nominative (SN) or accusative (DO). How do we decide? In a case like this, think about which makes the most sense.

    SN   DO V-t
1. Grāmen crūs tītillat.   *The grass tickles (his) leg.*

                  OR

    DO   SN V-t
2. Grāmen crūs tītillat.   *The leg tickles the grass.*

    Sentence #1 makes more sense!

C. TRANSLATE

Underline endings, label, and translate these sentences.

1. Arāneae tēlās nent. _____

2. Arānea ūna bēstiolam inlaqueābit. _____
_____

3. Lacerta provolābat inter saxa. _____
_____

4. Gryllus et cicāda folia mandūcant. _____
_____

5. Serpentēs lacertās sībilant. _____

6. Serpēns crūra nōn habet. _____

Lesson Thirty-Eight

7. Arānea crūra octō habet. _____

_____

D. DERIVATIVE DIGGING

List as many English words as you can think of that begin with the prefix *inter*. One word is given.

interact, _____

_____

Choose one derivative from your list and look it up in the dictionary. Write the word and its definition on the lines below:

WORD: _____

DEFINITION: _____

_____

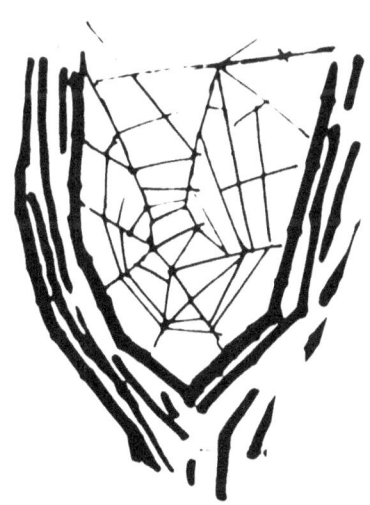

Lesson Thirty-Eight 227

20 List Twenty: Rock Quarry

VOCABULARY

Memorize the following Latin words and their translations. Know genitive forms and genders for nouns and the second principal parts of verbs.

Word	Derivative	Translation
1. lapis, lapidis, *m.*		*stone, rock*
2. lapicīdīnae, -ārum, *f.**		*rock quarry*
3. saxulum, -ī, *n.*		*little rock*
4. adamas, adamantis, *m.*		*diamond*
5. smaragdus, -ī, *m.* or *f.*		*emerald*
6. carbunculus, -ī., *m.*		*ruby*
7. later, lateris, *m.*		*brick*
8. lapsō, -āre		*slip, stumble*
9. lapidō, -āre		*throw stones at*
10. quassō, -āre		*break in pieces*
11. levō, -āre		*lift up*
12. tractō, -āre		*drag along, haul*
13. dūrus, -a, -um		*hard*
14. asper, aspera, asperum		*rough, uneven*
15. lapidōsus, -a, -um		*stony*

* *Lapicīdīnae* only appears in its plural form. It is similar to words like scissors or pants in which a plural word represents a singular noun.

REVIEW WORDS

1. līmo, -āre — *polish*
2. saxum, -ī, n. — *rock*
3. gemma, -ae, f. — *jewel*
4. plaustrum, -ī n. — *wagon*
5. fodicō, -āre — *dig*
6. mūrus, -ī, m. — *wall*
7. vīsito, -āre — *visit*
8. monstrō, -āre — *show*
9. cavum, -ī, n. — *hole*
10. aedificō*, -āre — *build*
11. est — *is*
12. altus, -a, -um — *high, tall*
13. liberi, -orum, m. — *children*
14. do, -are — *give*
15. parvus, -a, -um — *small, little*
16. pulcher, -chra, -chrum — *beautiful, handsome*
17. porto, -are — *carry*

Aedificio is from Logos Latin 1, but will also appear as a vocabulary word for this year on List 23.

230 List Twenty

39 Lesson Thirty-Nine: Rock Quarry

A. THIRD DECLENSION AND THE DATIVE CASE

Highlight the dative endings in the chants below.

FIRST DECLENSION

-a	-ae
-ae	-ārum
-ae	-īs
-am	-ās
-ā	-īs

SECOND DECLENSION

-us	-ī
-ī	-ōrum
-ō	-īs
-um	-ōs
-ō	-īs

THIRD DECLENSION

-x	-ēs
-is	-um
-ī	-ibus
-em	-ēs
-e	-ibus

You will remember that the dative case is used for indirect objects in Latin. Sentences containing indirect objects are called Pattern 3 sentences (SN V-t IO DO).

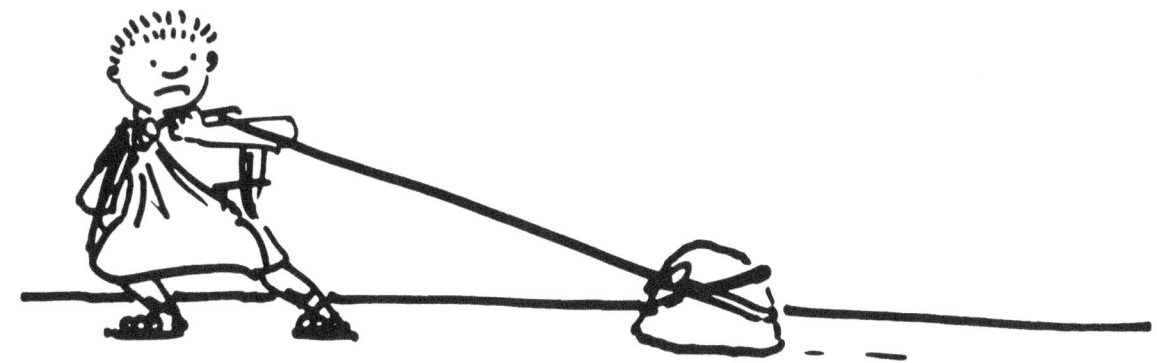

Lesson Thirty-Nine 231

B. PRACTICE

Identify the declensions (1st, 2nd, 2nd N., 3rd) of the nouns below. Then give the dative singular and plural forms of each. One is done as an example.

N.B. Find the base of the noun before adding the dative endings.

Word	Declension	Dative Singular	Dative Plural
1. lapis, lapidis	3rd	lapidī	lapidibus
2. saxulum, -ī			
3. lapicīdīnae, -ārum*		[no answer]	
4. adamās, adamantis			
5. carbunculus, -ī			
6. later, lateris			
7. smaragdus, -ī			

Lapicīdīnae only appears in the plural.

C. SENTENCE TRANSLATION

Translate these sentences. Some are Pattern 3 sentences containing indirect objects. <u>Underline</u> endings and label parts of speech.

1. Saxum Iūliō et Iūliae lapicīdīnās monstrat. _____

2. Saxum habitābat lapicīdīnās. _____

3. Saxum frātrem parvum habet. _____

4. Nōmen frātris est Saxulum.* _____

Lesson Thirty-Nine

5. Saxum et līberī laterēs portant. _____

6. Saxum et līberī Saxulō mūrum altum dant. _____

_____

Nomen means "name." *Fratris* is the genitive form of *frater* and is a possessive noun meaning "brother's."

D. MORE TRANSLATION

Translate these verbs into Latin. Pay attention to *who* is doing the action of the verb and *when* they are doing it. One is done as an example.

1. I was stumbling.   <u>lapsābam</u>

2. He will throw stones (at). _____

3. We will lift up. _____

4. You all were hauling. _____

_____

E. DERIVATIVE DIGGING

Look up the English derivative *lapidary* and write the definition on the lines below:

lapidary - _____

_____

40 Lesson Forty: Rock Quarry

A. REVIEW

<u>Underline</u> endings, label, and translate the sentences below. Each set of sentences begins with a verb and then builds Pattern 1, 2, and 3 sentences by adding nouns. The last sentence of each set adds an adjective.

Set #1

1. Fodicat. _____

2. Iūlius fodicat. _____

3. Iūlius cavum fodicat. _____

4. Iūlius lapidī cavum fodicat. _____

5. Iūlius lapidī cavum asperum fodicat. _____
_____

Set #2

1. Līmābit. _____

2. Saxum līmābit. _____

3. Saxum lapidem līmābit. _____

4. Saxum Iūliae lapidem līmābit. _____

5. Saxum Iūliae lapidem pulchrum līmābit. _____
_____

Set #3

1. Aedificābant. _____

2. Līberī aedificābant. _____

3. Līberī mūrum aedificābant. _____

4. Līberī Saxō mūrum aedificābant. _____

5. Līberī Saxō mūrum altum aedificābant. _____

_____

B. NOUN CASE PRACTICE

Match the noun cases at the right with the correct part(s) of speech at the left by writing the letter of the correct answer on the blank.

CASE	PART OF SPEECH
_____ Nominative	A. direct object, object of preposition
_____ Genitive	B. indirect object
_____ Dative	C. subject noun
_____ Accusative	D. sometimes object of preposition
_____ Ablative	E. possessive noun

C. TRANSLATE INTO LATIN

Now translate the English sentences below into Latin. Be sure to label parts of speech first and take care to use correct endings!

1. She gives. _____

Lesson Forty

2. Julia gives. _____

3. Julia gives a ruby. _____

4. Julia gives Rock a ruby. _____

5. Julia gives Rock a large ruby. _____
_____

D. TIDBIT

Roman jewelry tended to be made from glass or bronze. Precious gems and gold were only for the wealthy.

21 List Twenty-One: Parades & Pretending

VOCABULARY

Memorize the following Latin words and their translations. Know genitive forms and genders of nouns and the second principal parts of verbs.

Word	Derivative	Translation
1. mūsica, -ae, *f.*		*music*
2. imperātor, imperatōris, *m.*		*commander, emperor*
3. fīlia rēgis, *f.*		*princess*
4. corōna, -ae, *f.*		*crown*
5. scēptrum, -ī, *n.*		*scepter*
6. ōrātor, ōrātōris, *m.*		*speaker*
7. ōrātio, ōrātiōnis, *f.*		*speech*
8. trabea, -ae, *f.*		*robe of state*
9. gladiātor, gladiatōris, *m.*		*gladiator*
10. gladius, -ī, *m.*		*sword*
11. eques, equitis, *m.*		*horseman, knight*
12. pompa, -ae, *f.*		*parade*
13. saltātrīx, saltatrīcis, *f.*		*dancer*
14. carmen, carminis, *n.*		*song*
15. simulo, -āre		*pretend*

REVIEW WORDS

1. equus, -ī, *m.* — *horse*
2. senātor, senātōris, *m.* — *senator*
3. auscultō, -āre — *listen to*
4. possum, posse — *be able to*
5. pugnō, -āre — *fight*
6. equitō, -āre — *ride on horseback*
7. dō, -āre — *give*
8. senator, senatoris, *m.* — *senator*
9. rēx, rēgis, *m.* — *king*
10. luceō, -ēre — *shine* (from LL1 and will appear on List 22)

CHANT REVIEW

Review the third declension noun chants by filling in the missing boxes. Then check your work with your chant charts.

THIRD DECLENSION

-x	-ēs
-ī	-ibus
	-ibus

THIRD DECLENSION I-STEM

-is	-ēs
	-ibus
-em	
	-ibus

THIRD DECLENSION NEUTER

-x	-a
-is	
	-ibus

List Twenty-One

41 Lesson Forty-One: Parades & Pretending

A. GENITIVE REVIEW

Write in the genitive case endings for the declensions below.

FIRST DECLENSION

Nom.	-a	-ae
Gen.		
Dat.	-ae	-īs
Acc.	-am	-ās
Abl.	-ā	-īs

SECOND DECLENSION

Nom.	-us	-ī
Gen.		
Dat.	-ō	-īs
Acc.	-um	-ōs
Abl.	-ō	-īs

SECOND DECLENSION NEUTER

Nom.	-um	-a
Gen.		
Dat.	-ō	-īs
Acc.	-um	-a
Abl.	-ō	-īs

THIRD DECLENSION

Nom.	-x	-ēs
Gen.		
Dat.	-ī	-ibus
Acc.	-em	-ēs
Abl.	-e	-ibus

THIRD DECLENSION I-STEM*

Nom.	-is	-ēs
Gen.		
Dat.	-ī	-ibus
Acc.	-em	-ēs
Abl.	-e	-ibus

THIRD DECLENSION NEUTER

Nom.	-x	-a
Gen.		
Dat.	-ī	-ibus
Acc.	-x	-a
Abl.	-e	-ibus

*Which ending shows that a word is a third declension i-stem noun? _____

B. TRANSLATION

SINGULAR

Practice translating these phrases containing singular possessive nouns from the 3rd declension.

1. trabea imperatōris _____

2. gladius gladiatōris _____

Lesson Forty-One

3. equus equitis _____

4. carmen saltātrīcis _____

Challenge: sceptrum filiae regis _____

PLURAL

Now translate phrases containing plural possessive nouns from the third declension.

1. coronae imperātōrum _____

2. equī gladiātōrum _____

3. gladiī equitum _____

4. pompa saltātrīcum _____

Challenge: ōrātiōnēs ōrātōrum _____

C. SENTENCE TRANSLATION

Underline endings, label, and translate the sentences below. Circle any possessive nouns in the genitive case in both the Latin sentence and in your English translation.

1. Līberī et Saxum pompam imperatōris in Rōmā spectant. _____

2. Trabeae senatōrum limbōs purpureōs habent. _____

3. Gladiī gladiātōrum lucent. _____

4. Mīlitēs imperatōrem vigilant. _____

5. Iūlia et Claudia stolās saltātrīcum amant. _____

_____

6. Iūlius et Claudius equōs equitum amant. _____

_____

7. Parentēs Iūlī et Iuliae ōrātiōnem ōrātōris auscultant. _____

_____

D. LATIN QUESTIONS

Answer the questions below with the correct Latin word from List 21.

1. What does a *filia rēgis* wear on her head? _____

2. What does an *orator* give to an audience? _____

3. What does a *gladiator* fight with? _____

4. Who rides on an *equus*? _____

E. TIDBIT

Roman parades honored those who had returned from battle in triumph. This meant that the victorious leader had killed at least 5,000 troops or he and his army had won a war and were returning in peace. A parade could also be held to honor a very high elected official.

42 Lesson Forty-Two: Parades & Pretending

A. CIRCLE THE CORRECT ANSWERS

1. The second principal part of the verb is called the:
   a) subject noun   b) infinitive   c) preposition

2. The second principal part of the verb ends in **-re**. The ending **-re** means:
   a) from   b) in   c) to.

Now translate the second principal parts of the verbs below. One is done as an example.

1. levāre   to lift up

2. simulāre   _____

3. tractāre   _____

4. mandūcāre   _____

B. GENITIVE PRACTICE

Give the genitive singular and plural forms of the following nouns. Write the number of the declension each word is from. Be sure to find the base of the noun first.

WORD	GENITIVE SINGULAR	GENITIVE PLURAL	DECLENSION
1. ōrātio			
2. corōna			
3. gladius			

What part of speech is the genitive case in English? _____

C. DATIVE PRACTICE

Now give the dative singular and plural forms of the nouns below, as well as the declension. Find the base first!

WORD	DATIVE SINGULAR	DATIVE PLURAL	DECLENSION
1. trabea	_____	_____	_____
2. eques	_____	_____	_____
3. saltātrix	_____	_____	_____
4. saxum	_____	_____	_____

What part of speech is the dative case in English? _____

D. TRANSLATION

Underline endings, label, and translate the sentences below. Especially watch for nouns in the dative and genitive cases and for the infinitives (second parts) of verbs.

1. Iūlia et Claudia mūsicam auscultābant et saltābant. _____

2. Iūlius simulābat gladiatōrem pugnāre. _____

3. Claudius simulābat equitāre. _____

4. Iūlia Claudiō trabeam senatōris dābat. _____

Lesson Forty-Two

5. Puerī Saxō corōnam et scēptrum rēgis dābant. _____

_____

6. Līberī laetī simulābant ambulāre in pompā. _____

_____

E. TIDBIT

A person honored by a victory parade was called a *vir triumphalis*. After a *vir triumphalis* died, someone was hired to wear his death mask and purple robe of state in other parades.

Unit Seven Review

A. VOCABULARY

From memory, translate as many of these vocabulary words as you can. Then look up any you don't remember.

1. bēstiola, -ae _____

2. gryllus, -ī _____

3. crūs, crūris _____

4. inter _____

5. mandūcō, -āre _____

6. lapidōsus, -a, -um _____

7. tractō, -āre _____

8. adamās, adamantis _____

9. saxulum, -ī _____

10. dūrus, -a, -um _____

11. pompa, -ae _____

12. eques, equitis _____

13. imperātor, imperātōris _____

14. ōrātio, ōrātiōnis _____

15. filia rēgis _____

English to Latin

16. lift up   _____

17. slip, stumble   _____

18. grass   _____

19. sword   _____

20. song   _____

B. CHANT REVIEW

Fill in these noun chants.

THIRD DECLENSION (Regular)

-x	
-is	

THIRD DECLENSION I-STEM

-is	
-is	

THIRD DECLENSION NEUTER

-x	
-is	

Highlight the places where Third Neuter differs from regular third declension.

C. NOUN GENDER REVIEW

From memory, list the genders (masculine, feminine, neuter) of the following nouns. Then check your answers.

1. lapis, lapidis _____

2. saltātrīx, saltātrīcis _____

3. later, lateris _____

4. crūs, crūris _____

5. grāmen, grāminis _____

D. POSSESSIVE TRANSLATION

Translate these phrases containing possessive nouns:

1. grāmen serpentis _____

2. pompa imperātōris _____

3. ōrātiō ōrātōris _____

E. INDIRECT OBJECT TRANSLATION

Translate these Pattern 3 sentences containing indirect objects.

1. Cīcadae saltātrīcī carmen cantābant. _____

_____

2. Arānea gryllō tēlam nēbit inter arborēs. _____

_____

3. Fīlia rēgis gladiātōrī gladium dat. _____

_____

F. VERB TRANSLATION

Translate these second principal parts (or infinitives) of verbs.

1. provolāre _____

2. tītillāre _____

3. quassāre _____

G. SENTENCE TRANSLATION

Underline endings, label, and translate these sentences.

1. Bēstia serpēns prōvolat inter arborēs. _____

_____

2. Imperātor gladiātorī gladium equitis dat. _____

_____

3. Bēstiolae crūs saltātrīcis tītillābunt. _____

_____

H. DERIVATIVES

Write five derivatives from lists 19, 20, or 21 and give their Latin origins.

DERIVATIVE	LATIN ORIGIN
1. _____	_____
2. _____	_____
3. _____	_____
4. _____	_____
5. _____	_____

22 List Twenty-Two: Picnic

VOCABULARY

Memorize the following Latin words and their translations. Also learn the genitive endings for nouns and the second principal parts for verbs.

Word	Derivative	Translation
1. prandium, -ī, *n*.	_____	*lunch*
2. cāseus, -ī, *m*.	_____	*cheese*
3. pirum, -ī, *n*.	_____	*pear*
4. mensa secunda, *f*.	_____	*dessert*
5. sūcus, -ī, *m*.	_____	*juice*
6. sōl, sōlis, *m*.	_____	*sun*
7. ventus, -ī, *m*.	_____	*wind*
8. tonitrus, -ūs, *m*.*	_____	*thunder*
9. pluvia, -ae, *f*.	_____	*rain*
10. lutum, -ī, *n*.	_____	*mud*
11. silva, -ae, *f*.	_____	*forest*
12. lūceō, -ēre	_____	*shine, bright*
13. commūnicō, -āre	_____	*share*
14. sonō, -āre	_____	*sound*
15. per	_____	*through* (preposition w/acc.)

*This is from a declension we have not learned.

REVIEW WORDS

1. līberī, liberorum, *m.* — *children*
2. aqua, -ae, *f.* — *water*
3. libō, -are, *m.* — *sip, taste*
4. amīcus (amīca), -are, *f.* — *friend*
5. flō, -are — *blow*
6. videō, -ere — *see*
7. properō, -āre — *hurry*
8. dōmus, -us, *f.** — *home*
9. apportō, -āre — *bring*
10. potō, -are — *drink*
11. sedeō, -ēre — *sit*
12. terra, -ae, *f.* — *ground*

*Domus is from a declension we have not learned.

REVIEW CHANT

SUM CHANT – LINKING VERB (PRESENT TENSE)

sum - *I am*	sumus - *we are*
es - *you are*	estis - *you all are*
est - *he, she, it is*	sunt - *they are*

List Twenty-Two

43 Lesson Forty-Three: Picnic

A. LINKING VERBS — PRESENT TENSE

Review the Sum Chant and meanings below:

SUM CHANT — LINKING VERB (PRESENT TENSE)

sum - *I am*	sumus - *we are*
es - *you are*	estis - *you all are*
est - *he, she, it is*	sunt - *they are*

B. LINKING VERBS & PATTERN 4 SENTENCES

Study this Pattern 2 sentence :   SN   V-t   DO
                                    Julius shares the cheese.

  Does *cheese* mean the same thing as *Julius*? _____

  If the answer is no, then *cheese* is a direct object.

  What case do direct objects go in? _____

  This is a Pattern 2 sentence containing a subject noun, verb transitive and direct object.

Now study this sentence: SN   LV   ?
                           Julius is   the cheese.

  Does *cheese* mean the same thing as *Julius*? _____

  We could think of this sentence as a math problem.

  The linking verb can be called the equal sign: Julius = cheese

When a noun follows the linking verb and refers back to the subject noun it is called a *predicate noun* (not a direct object).

Go back to the sentence above and label the word *cheese* a PrN (predicate noun). Predicate nouns always go in the **nominative** case, just like subject nouns.

A sentence containing a subject noun, linking verb, and a predicate noun is called a *Pattern 4 sentence*.

N.B. Linking verbs do not take direct objects.

Now look at the same examples in Latin:

    SN   DO   V-t
    Iūlius cāse<u>um</u> commūnicat. (*Julius shares the cheese.*)

        What case is *cāseum* in? _____

    SN   LV   PrN
    Iūlius est cāse<u>us</u>. (*Julius is the cheese.*)

        What case is *cāseus* in? _____

C. TRANSLATION

Translate these Pattern 4 sentences containing linking verbs. Be sure to <u>underline</u> endings and label parts of speech (SN, LV, PrN).

1. Silva est lūcus. _____

2. Pluvia est aqua. _____

3. Uvae et baccae sunt mensae secundae. _____

_____

4. Cāseus est prandium. _____

Challenge question: In sentence #4, is the word *prandium* nominative or accusative?

_____

Lesson Forty-Three

D. TIDBIT

The *impluvium* was a hollowed out, sunken area in a Roman home located under an opening in the roof called the *atrium*. The atrium allowed sunlight and breezes to come into the house, but it also let in the rain which was collected in the impluvium. The impluvium was designed to drain off excess water as well. *Impluvium* is derived from what Latin word on List 22?

_____

_____

44 Lesson Forty-Four: Picnic

A. TRANSLATION

Label and translate the pairs of sentences below: PATTERN

1. Iūlius est amīcus. _____   _____

   Iūlius amīcum videt. _____   _____

2. Pluvia aquam apportat. _____   _____

   Pluvia est aqua. _____   _____

3. Iūlius et Iūlia sunt līberī. _____   _____

   Iūlius et Iūlia līberōs iuvant. _____   _____

   _____

Now, go back and identify the pattern of each sentence (is it Pattern 2 or 4?).

B. VERB REVIEW

Answer the questions below:

1. What case do direct objects go in? _____

2. What case do subject nouns go in? _____

3. What case do predicate nouns go in? _____

4. What kind of noun follows the linking verb? _____

5. Can linking verbs take direct objects? _____

C. STORY TRANSLATION

Translate the following story. <u>Underline</u> endings and label parts of speech.

1. Sōl lucet. _____

2. Iūlius, Iūlia, et amīcī prandium apportant ad silvam. _____

3. Līberī sedent in terrā et prandium commūnicant. _____

4. Lībant cāseum et potant sūcum. _____

5. Pirum est mēnsa secunda. _____

6. Tonitrus sonat et ventus flat per silvam! _____

7. Est* pluvia! _____

8. Līberī properant per lutum ad domum! _____

*<i>Est</i> means he, she, it is, but <i>est</i> can sometimes be translated as <i>there is</i>.

D. DERIVATIVE DIGGING

Look up the English word <i>resonate</i> in a dictionary and write its definition on the lines below. What is its Latin origin (the word it comes from) on List 22?

Definition: _____

Latin origin: _____

Lesson Forty-Four

23 List Twenty-Three: At the Seashore

VOCABULARY

Memorize the following Latin words and their translations. Also learn the genitive endings for nouns and the second principal parts for verbs.

Word	Derivative	Translation
1. ōceanus, -ī, *m.*		*ocean*
2. ōra maritima, -ae, *f.*		*seashore*
3. harēna, -ae, *f.*		*beach, sand*
4. unda, -ae, *f.*		*wave*
5. alga, -ae, *f.*		*seaweed*
6. gāvia, -ae, *f.*		*seagull*
7. hippocampus, -ī, *m.*		*seahorse*
8. umbra, -ae, *f.*		*shadow, shade*
9. umbella, -ae, *f.*		*parasol*
10. castellum, -ī, *m.*		*castle*
11. volō, -āre		*fly*
12. aedificō, -āre		*build*
13. flutō, -āre		*float*
14. ustulō, -āre		*burn*
15. trans		*over, across* (prep. with acc. case)

List Twenty-Three 263

REVIEW WORDS

1. in (w/abl.) — *in, on*
2. līberī, -ōrum, *m.* — *children*
3. fodicō, -āre — *dig*
4. habeō, -ēre — *have, hold*
5. dō, -āre — *give*
6. portō, -āre — *carry*
7. videō, -ēre — *see*
8. no, -are — *swim*

List Twenty-Three

45 Lesson Forty-Five: At the Seashore

A. LINKING VERBS – FUTURE TENSE

Review the present tense linking verb chant below and meanings below.

LINKING VERB (PRESENT TENSE)

sum - *I am*	sumus - *we are*
es - *you are*	estis - *you all are*
est - *he, she, it is*	sunt - *they are*

Now study the linking verb in the future tense.

LINKING VERB (FUTURE TENSE)*

erō – *I will be*	erimus - *we will be*
eris - *you will be*	eritis - *you all will be*
erit - *he, she, it will be*	erunt - *they will be*

*Be careful. This looks and sounds very similar to the Future Perfect Tense Verb Ending chant, but it is not! This is a linking verb, which means it can stand alone. The Future Perfect Tense verb endings can only be used when they are attached to a verb stem.

Now compare these Pattern 4 sentences containing subject nouns, linking verbs, and predicate nouns:

	SN LV PrN	SN LV PrN
Present Tense:	Iūlius est discipulus.	*Julius is a boy student.*

Does Julius mean the same thing as boy student? _____

	SN LV PrN	SN LV PrN
Future Tense:	Iūlius erit magister.	*Julius will be a teacher.*

Does Julius mean the same thing as teacher? _____

	SN LV PrN	SN LV PrN
Present Tense:	Iūlia est puella.	*Julia is a girl.*

Does Julia mean the same thing as girl? _____

	SN LV PrN	SN LV PrN
Future Tense:	Iūlia erit fēmina.	*Julia will be a woman.*

Does Julia mean the same thing as woman? _____

What case do predicate nouns go in? _____

What case do direct objects go in? _____

B. SENTENCE TRANSLATION

Translate the sentences below. Some are Pattern 2 sentences containing a SN, V-t, and DO. Others are Pattern 4 sentences which contain a SN, LV, and PrN. Be sure to underline endings and label parts of speech.

N.B. Sometimes the subject noun is hiding in the verb ending.

1. Ōra maritima est harēna. _____

2. Iūlius fodicābit in harēnā. _____

3. Sūmus līberī. _____

4. Erimus hippocampī! _____

5. Spectābimus hippocampōs. _____

6. Harēna erit castellum. _____

7. Iūlia et Saxum castellum aedificābunt. _____
_____

8. Iūlia portat umbellam. _____

9. Umbella erit umbra. _____

10. Umbella umbram dat. _____

C. TIDBIT

Did you know that the word *stella* can mean starfish? What else does *stella* mean?

_____
_____

46 Lesson Forty-Six: At the Seashore

A. TRANSLATION PRACTICE

Practice translating the linking verb in the present and future tenses. Identify the tense (present or future) of each verb. Try to do these from memory. Then look up the answers and write your corrections in red.

	TRANSLATION	TENSE
1. sumus		
2. erit		
3. erō		
4. sunt		
5. es		
6. estis		
7. erimus		
8. eris		
9. sum		
10. erunt		
11. eritis		
12. est		

B. STORY TRANSLATION

Translate the following story about a day at the beach. <u>Underline</u> endings and label parts of speech.

1. Sōl ūstulat. _____

2. Iūlius et Iūlia et amīcī ambulant ad ōram maritimam. _____
_____

3. Amīcī sunt Claudius et Claudia. _____

4. Umbellae sunt umbra. _____

5. Līberī flutant in undīs. _____

6. Gāvia volat in caelō et hippocampus nat in oceanō. _____
_____

7. Puellae ambulābunt trans harēnam et algam vidēbunt. _____
_____

8. Puerī castellum aedificābunt in harēnā. _____
_____

9. Līberī prandium habēbunt. _____
_____

C. ILLUSTRATION
Draw a picture of the day at the beach. Label your picture in Latin.

D. DERIVATIVES

Choose a derivative from List 23 and write its dictionary definition on the lines.

Word: _____

Definition: _____

_____

List Twenty-Four: Entertainment

VOCABULARY

Memorize the following Latin words and their translations. Also learn the genitive endings for nouns and the second principal parts for verbs.

Word	Derivative	Translation
1. circus, -ī, *m.*		*race course*
2. curriculum, -ī, *n.*		*race*
3. aurīga, -ae, *m.* or *f.*		*charioteer*
4. leo, leōnis, *m.*		*lion*
5. tīgris, tīgris, *m.*		*tiger*
6. elephantus, -i, *m.*		*elephant*
7. theātrum, -ī, *n.*		*theater*
8. lūdus scaenicus, -ī, *m.*		*a play*
9. scaena, -ae, *f.*		*stage*
10. actor, actōris, *m.*		*actor*
11. mīma, -ae, *f.*		*actress*
12. persōna, -ae, *f.*		*mask*
13. pugnō, -āre		*fight*
14. gestō, -āre		*wear*
15. rideō, -ēre		*laugh, smile*

REVIEW WORDS

1. specto, -āre — *look at, watch*
2. simulo, -āre — *pretend*
3. trans — *across (+acc.)*
4. īnfāns, īnfāntis, *m.* — *infant*
5. vir, -ī, *m.* — *man*
6. fēmina, -ae, *f.* — *woman*
7. terra, -ae, *f.* — *land*
8. līberī, -ōrum, *m.* — *children*
9. aedificium, -ī, *n.* — *building*
10. ambulō, -āre — *walk*
11. leo, leōnis, *m.* — *lion*
12. tīgris, tīgris, *m.* — *tiger*
13. elephantus, -ī, *m.* — *elephant*
14. simulō, -āre — *pretend*

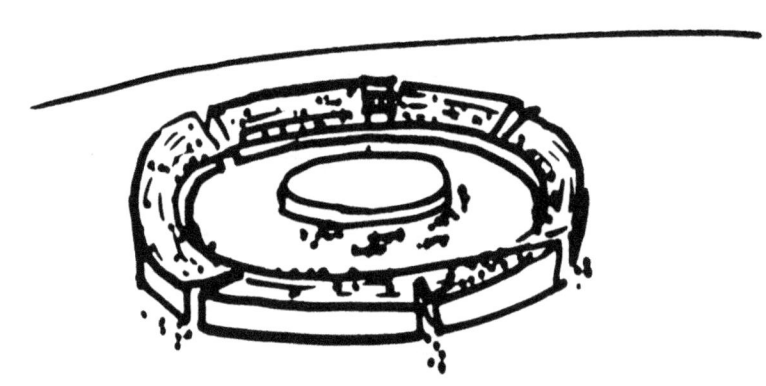

47 Lesson Forty-Seven: Entertainment

A. LINKING VERBS – IMPERFECT TENSE

Fill in the linking verb chants below and translate:

LINKING VERB (PRESENT TENSE)

sum -	

LINKING VERB (FUTURE TENSE)

erō -	

Now study the linking verb in the imperfect tense:

LINKING VERB (IMPERFECT TENSE)

eram - *I was*	erāmus - *we were*
erās - *you were*	erātis - *you all were*
erat - *he, she, it was*	erant - *they were*

Remember, these are not the same as the Future Perfect and Pluperfect verb endings which are included in the verb chants.

Practice writing the linking verb in the imperfect tense and its meanings below:

eram -	

N.B. *Tense* simply means the time when something happens. The word *being* is optional for the Imperfect linking verb.

Look at the examples below to help you think about linking verb tenses:

	SN LV PrN	SN LV PrN
IMPERFECT TENSE:	Iūlius erat īnfāns.	*Julius was a baby.* (in the past)
	Iūlia erat īnfāns.	*Julia was a baby.*

	SN LV PrN	SN LV PrN
PRESENT TENSE:	Iūlius est puer.	*Julius is a boy.* (in the present)
	Iūlia est puella.	*Julia is a girl.*

	SN LV PrN	SN LV PrN
FUTURE TENSE:	Iūlius erit vir.	*Julius will be a man.* (in the future)
	Iūlia erit fēmina.	*Julia will be a woman.*

N.B. Remember, linking verbs do not take direct objects. Predicate nouns go with linking verbs. Like subject nouns, predicate nouns go in the nominative case.

B. TRANSLATION PRACTICE

Practice translating the linking verb in the present, imperfect, and future tenses in the sentences below. Label parts of speech.

1. Aedificium est theātrum. _____

2. Iūlius erit āctor. _____

3. Fēmina nōn erat mīma. _____

Lesson Forty-Seven

4. Līberī erunt elephantī in ludō scaenicō. _____

_____

5. Virī sunt aurīgae. _____

6. Terra erat circus. _____

7. Eritis mīmae. _____

8. Eram actor in scaenā. _____

C. TIDBIT

Roman theater often imitated Greek plays. However, the Romans tended to prefer comedies. Colors let the audience know what sort of person the actor was portraying. For example, a purple robe meant the character was a rich man. An actor in a yellow robe was playing a woman (this was before women were allowed to act on stage), and an actor wearing a yellow tassel represented a god.

48 Lesson Forty-Eight: Entertainment

A. REVIEW QUESTIONS

Translate the following Latin questions. <u>Underline</u> endings and label parts of speech. Highlight or circle the **-ne** question ending. Remember to start your question with an appropriate helping verb.

1. Spectatne aurīga curriculum? _____

2. Pugnābitne leō elephantum? _____

3. Mīmane personam gestābat? _____

4. Simulābimusne pugnāre in scaenā? _____

5. Potesne ridēre in theatrō? _____

6. Ambulābatne āctor trans scaenam? _____

B. LINKING VERB TRANSLATION

Translate these linking verbs from the present, imperfect, and future tenses:

1. eritis _____

2. sumus _____

3. erant _____

4. eram _____

5. es _____

6. erit _____

C. QUESTION TRANSLATION

Now translate questions containing the linking verb. <u>Underline</u> endings and label parts of speech. The first one is done as an example.

   LV SN PrN
1. Erit<u>ne</u> Iūli<u>a</u> mīm<u>a</u>? Will Julia be an actress? _____

2. Eratne vir aurīga? _____

3. Estisne elephantī in ludō scaenicō? _____

_____

4. Sūmusne aurīgae? _____

D. TIDBIT

Chariot racing was the most popular sport in ancient Rome. The Circus Maximus held nearly 250,000 people. Spectators would cheer on their favorite charioteer, shouting, *"Aurīga! Aurīga!"*

Lesson Forty-Eight

Unit Eight Review

A. VOCABULARY

From memory, translate as many of these vocabulary words as you can. Then look up any you don't remember.

1. prandium, -ī   _____
2. pirum, -ī   _____
3. sūcus, -ī   _____
4. ventus, -ī   _____
5. pluvia, -ae   _____
6. silva, -ae   _____
7. communicō, -āre   _____
8. trans   _____
9. flutō, -āre   _____
10. castellum, -ī   _____
11. umbra, -ae   _____
12. alga, -ae   _____
13. hippocampus, -ī   _____
14. curriculum, -ī   _____
15. leō, leōnis   _____
16. scaena, -ae   _____

17. persōna, -ae _____

18. circus, -ī _____

19. gestō, -āre _____

20. rideō, -ēre _____

B. LINKING VERBS

Fill in the linking verbs and meanings in the present, imperfect, and future tenses.

LINKING VERB (PRESENT TENSE)

sum -	

LINKING VERB (IMPERFECT TENSE)

eram -	

LINKING VERB (FUTURE TENSE)

ero -	

C. TRANSLATION

Translate the following sentences. <u>Underline</u> endings and label parts of speech.

1. Tonitrus sonābat trans harēnam. _____

2. Leō elephantum pugnābit. _____

3. Communicantne līberī prandium? _____

4. Ūstulāte castellum. _____

5. Possumus gestāre personās. _____

D. MORE TRANSLATION

Translate the following Pattern 4 sentences containing linking verbs and predicate nouns.

1. Ōra maritima erat harēna _____

2. Iūlius et Claudius erunt aurīgae. _____

3. Estne Iūlia mīma? _____

4. Sunt hippocampī. _____

5. Erāmus līberī. _____

E. DERIVATIVES

Write derivatives for the following Latin words:

1. scaena _____

2. rideō _____

3. mīma _____

4. alga _____

5. harēna _____

6. trans _____

7. ventus _____

8. sōl _____

9. luceō _____

10. per _____

F. MACARONIC STORY

Write a short macaronic story using at least ten vocabulary words from Lists 22, 23, and 24. Underline the Latin words.

_____

_____

_____

_____

_____

_____

_____

_____

_____

49 Lesson Forty-Nine: Review Lists 1-9 and Units 1-3

A. VOCABULARY

Read through Lists 1 - 9 and then fill in as many of the following words as you can from memory. Then look up any you don't remember.

1. discipulus _____
2. liber _____
3. fabula _____
4. frater _____
5. ad _____
6. gallus _____
7. porca _____
8. aqua _____
9. hortus _____
10. urbs _____
11. ecclēsia _____
12. convīvium _____
13. medicus _____
14. quod _____
15. via _____

16. magistra _____
17. amīcus _____
18. lūdus _____
19. servus _____
20. vacca _____
21. faenum _____
22. ager _____
23. oleum _____
24. cavum _____
25. aedificium _____
26. dōnum _____
27. annus _____
28. lingua _____
29. morbus _____
30. in(w/abl.) _____

B. VERB TRANSLATION

Use your verb charts to review the present, imperfect, and future tense verb endings. Then underline endings on these verbs from lists 1 - 9 and translate.

1. recitāmus _____
2. habēbis _____
3. ambulābō _____
4. secat _____
5. potant _____
6. florēbunt _____
7. stabat _____
8. flās _____
9. dolēbātis _____

10. rogābant _____
11. numerātis _____
12. apportābāmus _____
13. dābimus _____
14. curābam _____
15. compleō _____
16. errābit _____
17. ornābās _____
18. devorābitis _____

C. INFINITIVE TRANSLATION

Translate these infinitives (or second principal parts) of the verbs below. One is done as an example.

1. cubāre   to lie down
2. exclamāre _____
3. occultāre _____
4. fodicāre _____

D. STEM REVIEW

Find the stem of these verbs by removing the infinitive ending. One is done as an example.

INFINITIVE	STEM
1. laborāre	labora
2. arāre	_____
3. vīsitāre	_____

E. COMMANDS

The verb stem can also be used as a singular command. One command is translated as an example. Translate the other two.

1. Laborā in horreō.   Work in the barn.

2. Arā hortum.   _____

3. Vīsitā forum.   _____

To make a command plural, add _____ to the singular command.

F. CONJUGATE & TRANSLATE

Conjugate and translate the verb *possum* in the box below:

possum - *I am able*	

Now translate sentences containing forms of *possum* and infinitives. Underline endings and label parts of speech. One example is done for you.

    SN   DO   V-t   INF
1. Discipula historiam potest recitāre.   The girl student is able to recite history.

2. Ancillae cēnam possunt parāre. _____

3. Possumus faenum struāre. _____

Lesson Forty-Nine   287

G. FILL IN THE BLANKS

To form a question in Latin, the ending _____ is added to the _____ word in the sentence.

Usually, the first word in a Latin question is the _____ .

Now underline endings, label, and translate these questions into English. Remember to start your English question with an appropriate helping verb. An example is done for you.

      V-t   SN DO
1. Mulgēbatne Iūlia vaccam? _Was Julia milking the cow?_____

2. Tondēbuntne Iūlius et Claudius ovēs? _____
_____

3. Aegrotatne Claudia? _____

50 Lesson Fifty: Review Lists 10-18 and Units 4-6

A. VOCABULARY

Read through Lists 10 - 18 and translate as many of the following words as you can from memory. Then look up any you don't remember.

1. urbs _____
2. aedificium _____
3. fūmus _____
4. lingua _____
5. morbus _____
6. ruber _____
7. aurum _____
8. armilla _____
9. fenestra _____
10. primus _____
11. praemium _____
12. spēlunca _____
13. ferus _____
14. fluvius _____
15. quartus _____

16. via _____
17. annus _____
18. candēla _____
19. medicamentum _____
20. coma _____
21. magnus _____
22. margārita _____
23. mūrus _____
24. rotundus _____
25. decimus _____
26. laurea _____
27. hodiē _____
28. bene _____
29. repente _____
30. altus _____

B. VERB TRANSLATION

Use your verb charts to reivew the present, imperfect, and future tense verb endings. Then underline endings and translate these verbs from Lists 10 - 18.

1. errātis _____
2. stābunt _____
3. flō _____
4. occultās _____
5. dolēmus _____
6. venditābō _____
7. nuntiant _____
8. nabāmus _____
9. redundat _____

10. exclamābās _____
11. saltābimus _____
12. ornābam _____
13. celebrābātis _____
14. limābit _____
15. iactābat _____
16. fugitābis _____
17. firmābitis _____
18. exspectābant _____

C. GENITIVE CASE (POSSESSIVE NOUN) REVIEW

Underline endings, label, and translate these sentences containing possessive nouns.

1. Iūlia lībum nātāle Iūlī ornat. _____

_____

2. Claudius pilam Claudiae per fenestrām iactat. _____

_____

3. Pāter sīcas puerōrum limābit. _____

_____

Lesson Fifty

D. DATIVE CASE (INDIRECT OBJECT) REVIEW

Underline endings, label, and translate these sentences containing indirect objects.

1. Medicus Iūliae et Iūlio pilulas dat. _____

_____

2. Magistra Saxō praemium adiūdicābat. _____

_____

3. Tabernārius puellīs armillās venditābit._____

_____

E. ADJECTIVE REVIEW

Adjectives match the nouns they describe in **gender, number**, and **case**. Tell whether each term below is a gender, number, or case. One is done for you.

1. masculine   gender_____

2. nominative   _____

3. genitive   _____

4. plural   _____

5. feminine   _____

6. ablative   _____

7. singular   _____

8. accusative   _____

9. neuter   _____

10. dative   _____

N.B. Adjectives often follow the noun they describe.

F. SENTENCE TRANSLATION

Underline endings, label, and translate these sentences containing adjectives.

1. Claudia pulchra stolam roseam gestat. _____

_____

2. Tabernārius parvus margaritās magnās venditābat. _____

_____

G. ORDINAL & CARDINAL NUMBERS

Write out the ordinal numbers in order in Latin. The first one is done as an example.

1. first   prīmus, -a, -um
2. second   _____
3. third   _____
4. fourth   _____
5. fifth   _____
6. sixth   _____
7. seventh   _____
8. eighth   _____
9. ninth   _____
10. tenth   _____

Fill in the missing cardinal numbers: unus, _____ , _____ , quattuor, quīnque, sex, _____ , _____ , novem, _____ .

H. MORE SENTENCE TRANSLATION

Underline endings, label, and translate these sentences.

1. Duo puerī pilam quartam trans murum septimum calcitrant _____

_____

2. Secunda puella monumentum decimum spectābit. _____

_____

Challenge Sentence: Iūlia et Iūlius tria monumenta spectābant. _____

_____

51 Lesson Fifty-One: Review Lists 19-24 and Units 7-8

A. VOCABULARY

Read through Lists 19-24 and translate as many of the following words as you can from memory. Then look up any you don't remember.

1. bēstiola _____
2. arānea _____
3. asper _____
4. imperātor _____
5. gladius _____
6. ventus _____
7. umbra _____
8. alga _____
9. persona _____
10. mīma _____
11. crūs _____
12. lapis _____
13. carbunculus _____
14. corōna _____
15. sōl _____
16. silva _____
17. harēna _____
18. aurīga _____
19. curriculum _____
20. tonitrus _____

B. VERB TRANSLATION

Use your verb charts to review the present, imperfect, and future tense verb endings. Then <u>underline</u> endings and translate these verbs from Lists 19-24.

1. gestābant _____
2. ridētis _____

3. pugnābimus _____   4. volābat _____

5. flutās _____   6. ustulābō _____

7. sonābam _____   8. lucēbis _____

9. communicat _____   10. saltābāmus _____

11. lapsābitis _____   12. levant _____

13. tractābātis _____   14. quassāmus _____

15. manducābitis _____   16. provolābās _____

17. neō _____   18. titillābit _____

C. LINKING VERB TRANSLATION

Practice translating the linking verbs below in the present, imperfect, and future tenses. Italicized words are in English and need to be translated into Latin.

1. sum _____   10. eras _____

2. erit _____   11. es _____

3. erat _____   12. erimus _____

4. est _____   13. erāmus _____

5. eritis _____   14. sumus _____

6. erātis _____   15. erunt _____

7. estis _____   16. erant _____

8. *they are* _____   17. *I was* _____

9. *I will be* _____   18. *you will be* _____

Lesson Fifty-One

D. SENTENCE TRANSLATION

Underline endings, label, and translate the following sentence sets. Each sentence builds upon the one before it. Possible sentence "ingredients" include: V, V-t, LV, SN, DO, IO, PrN, PNA, Adj, P, OP. Sentence pattern numbers are given in parenthesis.

Set #1

1. (P1) Arānea net. _____

2. (P2) Arānea telam net. _____

3. (P3) Arānea bēstiolae telam net. _____

4. (P3) Arānea bēstiolae telam net inter lapidēs. _____
_____

5. (P3) Arānea bēstiolae telam net inter lapidēs durōs. _____
_____

6. (P4) Bēstiola est cicāda. _____

7. (P4) Bēstiola est cicāda arāneae. _____

Set #2

1. (P1) Tigris cantābat. _____

2. (P2) Tigris carmen cantābat. _____

3. (P3) Tigris elephantō carmen cantābat. _____
_____

4. (P3) Tigris elephantō carmen foedum cantābat. _____
_____

5. (P3) Tigris elephanto carmen foedum gryllī cantābat. _____

_____

6. (P3) Tigris elephanto carmen foedum gryllī cantābat per silvam. _____

_____

7. (P4) Eratne tigris leo? _____

8. (P4) Tigris non erat leo! _____

Set #3 — Challenge Set

Translate these sentences into Latin. Be sure to label the English sentences first.

N.B. The Latin word for *leg* is in third declension <u>neuter</u>.

1. (P1) The lizard will tickle. _____

2. (P2) The lizard will tickle the leg. _____

3. (P2) The lizard will tickle Julius's leg. _____

4. (P3) Julius will build the lizard a castle. _____

5. (P4) The lizard is a reptile. _____

52 Lesson Fifty-Two: Tres Capri Gruff

TRANSLATE "THE THREE BILLY GOATS GRUFF" INTO ENGLISH

There is a special glossary at the end of this story on p. 302.

1. Ōlim erant trēs caprī. _____

2. Nōmen capriōrum erat "Gruffus". _____
_____

3. Trēs Caprī Gruffi grāmen in colle trans rīvum vidēbant. _____
_____

4. Erat pōns trans rivum. _____

5. Trollus foedus habitābat sub pontē. _____
_____

6. Trollus habet nasum longum et oculōs magnōs. _____
_____

7. Primus Caper Gruffus erat parvus. _____

8. Caper Gruffus parvus ambulābat trans pōntem. _____
_____

9. Pōns, "Trippus, trappus! Trippus, trappus!" inquit. _____
_____

10. Trollus rogābat: "Quis ambulat trans pōntem meum?" _____

_____

11. Prīmus Caper Gruffus, "Sum Prīmus Caper Gruffus," inquit. _____

_____

_____

12. Trollus clamabat: "Tē devorābō!" _____

_____

13. "Exspectā," inquit Primus Caper Gruffus, "meum frātrem maiorem." _____

_____

_____

14. Secundus Caper Gruffus ambulābat trans pōntem. _____

_____

15. Pōns, "Trippus, trappus! Trippus, trappus!" inquit. _____

_____

16. Trollus rogābat: "Quis ambulābat trans pōntem meum?" _____

_____

17. Caper, "Sum Secundus Caper Gruffus," inquit. _____

_____

18. Trollus clamābat: "Tē devorābo!" _____

_____

19. "Exspectā," inquit Secundus Caper Gruffus, "meum frātrem maximum." _____

20. Tertius Caper Gruffus ambulābat trans pōntem. _____

21. Pōns, "Trippus, trappus! Trippus, trappus!" inquit. _____

22. Trollus rogābat: "Quis ambulābat trans pōntem meum?" _____

23. Caper, "Sum Tertius Caper Gruffus," inquit. _____

24. Trollus clamābat, "Tē devorābo!" _____

25. Caper Gruffus Maximus Trollum oppugnābat et necābat. _____

26. Trēs Caprī Gruffī gramen manducābant in colle et pinguēscēbant. _____

Lesson Fifty-Two 301

GLOSSARY FOR THE STORY

1. ōlim — *once* (once upon a time)
2. erat, erant — *was, were* (can be translated as *there was, there were*)
3. caper, caprī, m. — *male goat*
4. collis, collis, m. — *hill*
5. rīvus, -ī, m. — *stream*
6. pōns, pōntis, m. — *bridge*
7. habitō, -are — *live, dwell*
8. sub — *under* (preposition w/abl.)
9. nasus, -ī, m. — *nose*
10. oculus, -ī, m. — *eye*
11. "Trippus, trappus!" — *"Trip, trap!"* (representing the sound the bridge makes when the goats cross)
12. inquit — *he, she, it said* (This word is only used with direct quotations and it is never used before the quote. Instead, it is inserted in the quote.)
13. Quis? — *Who?*
14. Tē — *you* in the accusative singular (from the Ego Chant)
15. meus, mea, meum — *my*
16. māior — *larger, bigger*
17. maximus, -a, -um — *largest, biggest*
18. oppūgnō, āre — *attack*
19. necō, -āre — *kill*
20. pinguescō, ēre — *grow fat*
21. nōmen, nominis, n. — *name*

ACTIVITY PAGES

A List One: Matching Game

Draw a line from the Latin word to its English translation. When you are done, choose your favorite words and draw a picture of them below.

Latin	English
rogō	arithmetic
discipulus	book
historia	girl student
recitō	male teacher
magister	recite
littera	female teacher
discipula	history
līber	boy student
magistra	letter
arithmētica	ask

A List Two: Draw a Classroom

Translate the following words into English, then illustrate the scene below that includes at least six of the items from the list. Label them in Latin when you are finished. Note: One word is from List 1, and one is a review word.

mēnsa	_____	tabula	_____
sella	_____	amīcus	_____
amīca	_____	stylus	_____
charta	_____	magister	_____

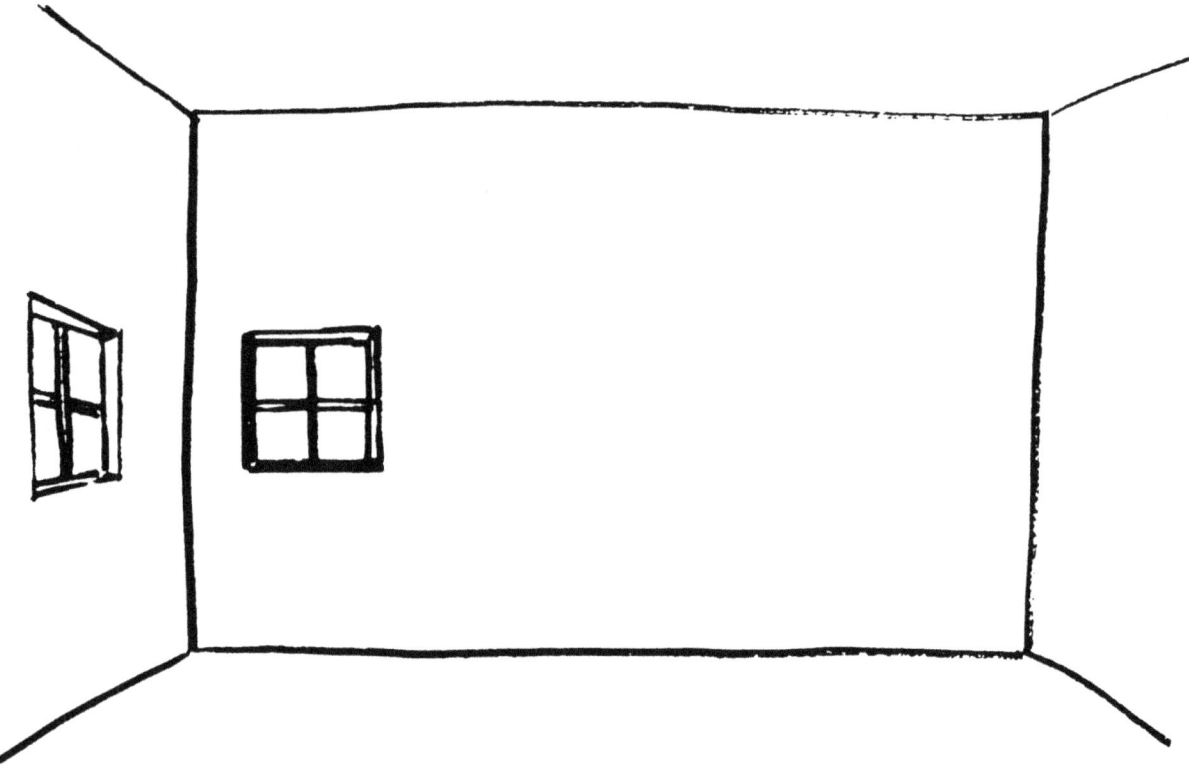

306 Activity Pages

A List Three: Word Search

Search the grid and circle the **Latin translation** of the English words. Words may be spelled forwards, backwards, upwards, downwards, or diagonally.

```
V L K F Q A M B U L O
W R K H R S U C O F Q
A T M R G A K D O X L
N N W N K F T T M X J
L I E R R Y R E F N A
R V N C S O R O R N S
E I O V P N I R C T E
T S R P I J E I L F R
A I A N D T L F X Q V
M T P Y A L O Y B A U
J O J P A R Q N D Z S
```

mother _____   father _____
sister _____   brother _____
slave, servant _____   maidservant _____
hearth, fireplace _____   dinner, meal _____
prepare _____   bring _____
walk _____   invite _____
visit _____   to, toward _____
in, on _____

Activity Pages 307

A List Four: Coloring a Farm

Color this picture of a farmyard and label the drawings in Latin.

A List Five: Comic Strip

Use the squares provided below to draw a macaronic-style comic strip about Julia, Julius, their grandfather, and Saxum. Their grandfather owns a farm. You must use at least five words from List 5.

A List Six: Crossword Puzzle

Fill in the Latin translations of the English words by following the ACROSS and DOWN clues. Match the number of the clue to the numbered boxes going in that direction.

ACROSS
2 grape _____
5 basket _____
6 dig _____
9 berry _____
13 garden _____
14 hole _____
15 bloom, flourish _____

DOWN
1 branch _____
3 prune _____
4 olive, olive tree _____
7 olive oil _____
8 grove _____
10 with _____
11 flask, bottle _____
12 fill up _____

List Seven: Postcard from Rome

You and your family have traveled to the beautiful and ancient city of Rome. Write a macaronic-style postcard using at least five words from List 7. When you are done, illustrate the front of your postcard.

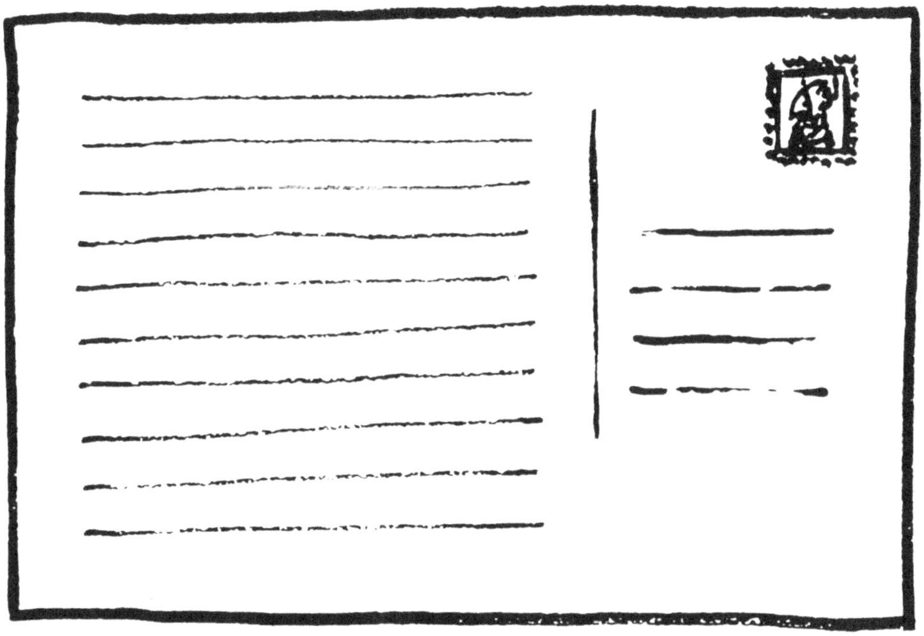

List Eight: Color a Birthday Party

Julia is throwing a birthday party for Julius. Color the picture and use the words from List 8 to label it.

A List Nine: Word Search

Search the grid and circle the **Latin translation** of the English words. Words may be spelled forwards, backwards, upwards, downwards, or diagonally.

```
V H R T Y P T V T X X Q I
T X N D Z A U G N I L M H
D E V O R O L T B P G L C
W K L H R E Y M O N E O A
M E D I C A M E N T U M M
O B K T J C M S A P L K O
T E U V Y L U T E I O X T
M S L O W C T K G L S W S
Z O B O I Z S Y R U T C R
Q U R D D Q U Z O L E J O
C U E B Q X R X T A N F L
Z M O Y U J F T O C D X O
T X V D R S G V W L E Z D
```

piece _____
sickness _____
bed _____
grieve _____
warn _____

doctor _____
stomach ache _____
tongue _____
lie down _____
stick out _____

medicine _____
pill _____
be sick _____
swallow _____
because _____

List Ten: Color-by-Number

Follow the directions to finish this Color-by-number. The numbers correspond to the Latin words for colors. If you want, you can translate the Latin into English first on the lines provided.

1=caeruleus
2=ruber
3=albus
4=flāvus
5=fulvus
6=niger

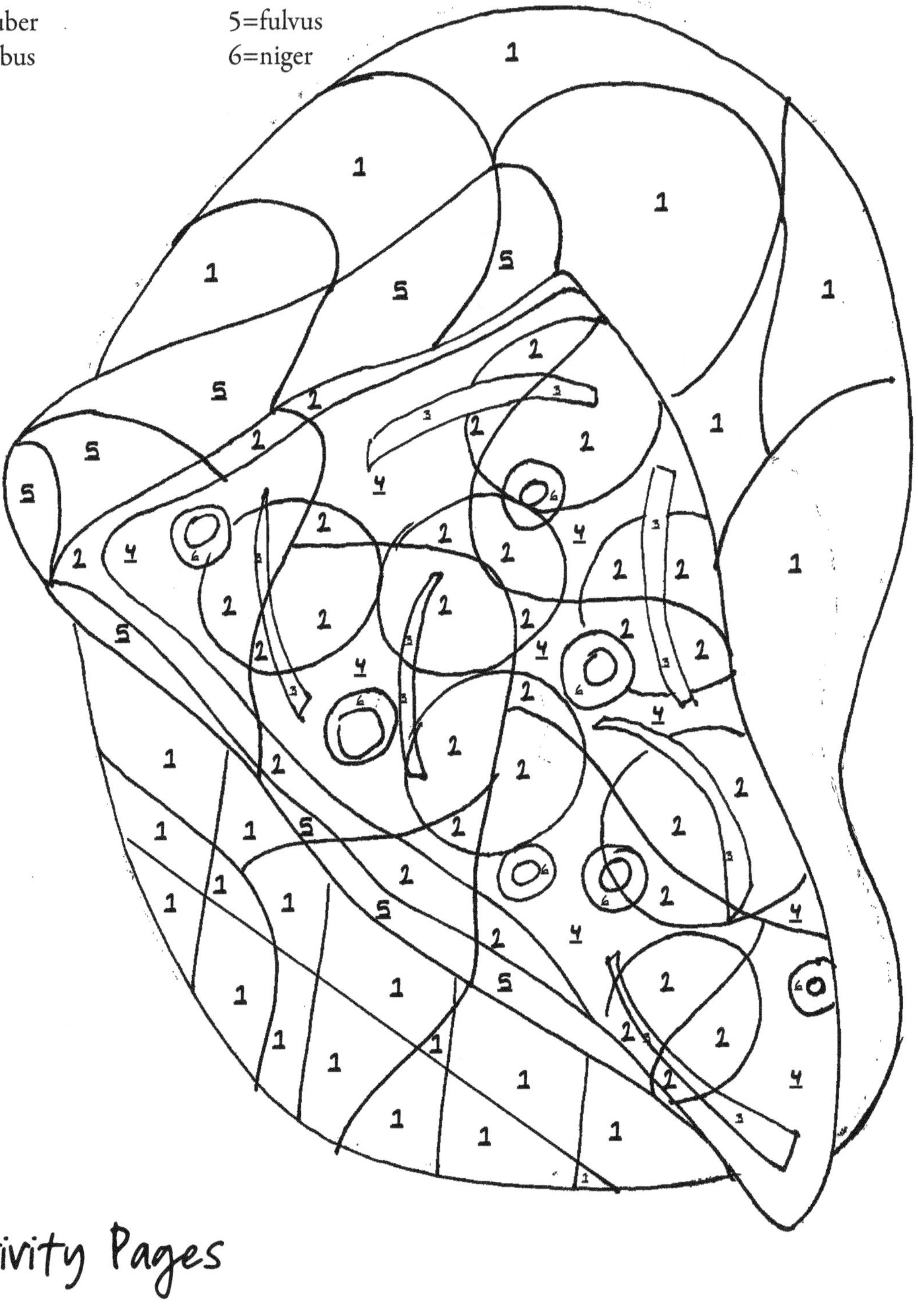

Activity Pages

A List Eleven: Anagram

For this activity you will have to unscramble the English words and translate them into Latin. Write the English words in the first column of blanks and then write the Latin translation in the second column. Choose your favorite and draw a picture at the bottom of the page.

racbetel _____ _____

rpepeekosh _____ _____

welej _____ _____

relpa _____ _____

ignr _____ _____

logd _____ _____

tefabuilu _____ _____

lugy _____ _____

sholip _____ _____

List Twelve: Crossword Puzzle

Fill in the Latin translation of the English words below by following the ACROSS and DOWN clues. Match the number of the clue to the numbered boxes going in that direction.

ACROSS
1 ball _____
3 through _____
6 window _____
7 wall _____
8 slow _____
9 angry _____
12 shout _____
13 wide _____

DOWN
2 high, tall _____
3 cart _____
4 kick _____
5 athletic field _____
10 round _____
11 throw _____
12 fast, swift _____

A List Thirteen: Color the Jewels

Julius and Julia are looking at jewels in a store window. Counting left to right, follow the directions to color the jewels correctly. Translate the ordinal numbers from the Latin into English on the blanks provided.

COLOR THIS JEWEL . . .   THIS COLOR

septimus _____   niger   _____

secundus _____   flavus   _____

quintus _____   niger   _____

sextus _____   aurum   _____

nomus _____   caeruleus _____

decimus _____   ruber   _____

tertius _____   roseus   _____

quartus _____   albus   _____

octavus _____   ruber   _____

primus _____   caeruleus _____

Activity Pages 317

A List Fourteen: Word Search

Search the grid and circle the **Latin translation** of the English words. Words may be spelled forwards, backwards, upwards, downwards, or diagonally.

```
M D K A S T O R R Y Z S
S S U S O M I N A G R U
A E A F U G I T O A G R
R X T C M H N Z C K T E
C S I M C L Q N Z H N F
X P M E B U U T O T G R
R E I T X L R D I R R O
C C D N E P I A R R C N
W T U P V E L P T O E T
N O S Q T K C O V U L H
L Z T H E S A U R U S D
D O E N I T E R W O L K
```

wild animal _____	cave _____
treasure _____	careful _____
fearful _____	courageous _____
today _____	yesterday _____
tomorrow _____	call _____
stand near _____	wait for _____
hold back _____	flee from _____
explore _____	

Activity Pages

List Fifteen: Macaronic Story

Write a macaronic story below on the spaces provided. Be sure to use at least ten Latin words. Focus on the words from Lists 14 & 15 and write an adventure story. Underline the Latin words you use.

List Sixteen: Solve a Crime

Robbers have stolen something important in ancient Rome. You are a detective trying to solve the crime. Different people keep telling you bits and pieces of the story. To solve the crime, translate the clues and put them in order using the Latin word for the ordinal number.

_____   Praedō argentum et aurum in fruticē occultat. _____

_____

_____   Praedō domum parentum astat. _____

_____

_____   Mater cubābat in lectō. _____

_____

_____   Canis praedonem videt. _____

_____

_____   Canis latrat et soror ululat. _____

_____

_____   Praedō gemmas pātrīs exspoliābit. _____

_____

_____   Praedō citus a domō fugitat. _____

_____

_____   Pāter gemmas domō comportābat. _____

_____

List Seventeen: Crossword

Fill in the Latin translation of the English words by following the ACROSS and DOWN clues. Match the number of the clue to the numbered boxes going in that direction.

ACROSS
1 citizen _____
5 condemn _____
6 officer _____
9 greedy _____
11 guilty _____
13 order _____
14 judge, juror _____
15 testimony _____

DOWN
2 opinion _____
3 soldier _____
4 witness _____
7 prison _____
8 guard _____
10 trial, court _____
12 send away _____

A List Eighteen: Vocabulary Drawing

Draw as many pictures from this week's word list as you can. Label your pictures in Latin.

A) List Nineteen: Matching Game

Translate the words on the lines provided. Then draw a line between the Latin word and the corresponding picture. The words are from the list 19 and the review list. Color in the pictures when you are done.

bēstiola _____   bēstia serpēns _____

cicāda _____   gryllus _____

arānea _____   tela _____

serpēns _____   lacerta _____

grāmen _____

Activity Pages   323

List Twenty: Word Search

Search the grid and circle the **Latin translation** of the English words. Words may be spelled forwards, backwards, upwards, downwards, or diagonally.

```
O N S U S O D I P A L R Q
S D H P G C M L M T E L D
S N O O S P A L F A S V U
A A V D L L J C N H M J R
U D D A I K L I M A A K U
Q T T A O P D V S H R D S
L E R V M I A P S G A G K
R V E A C A E L I Z G T R
J L T I C R S Z P Y D B K
H H P W N T C X A L U K H
B A Y J X T O P L G S H M
L C A R B U N C U L U S H
G C W S A X U L U M D G H
```

stone, rock _____ rock quarry _____
little rock _____ diamond _____
emerald _____ ruby _____
brick _____ to slip, stumble _____
to throw stones at _____ to break in pieces _____
to lift up _____ to drag along, haul _____
hard _____ rough, uneven _____
stony _____

List Twenty-One: Macaronic Fairytale

Write a macronic story below on the spaces provided. Be sure to use at least five Latin words. Focus on the words from this week's list by writing a fairytale. Underline the Latin words you use.

A List Twenty-Two: Anagram

For this activity you will have to unscramble the English words and translate them into Latin. Write the English words in the first column of blanks and then write the Latin translation in the second column. Choose your favorite and draw a picture at the bottom of the page.

ENGLISH   **LATIN**

pare   _____   _____

uns   _____   _____

diwn   _____   _____

rani   _____   _____

neruthd   _____   _____

cujie   _____   _____

gruthoh   _____   _____

eseche   _____   _____

A List Twenty-Three: Draw the Seashore

Illustrate and label (in Latin) a picnic at the beach. You can look at word list 21 & 22 for ideas of things to draw and label.

Twenty-Four: Macaronic Story

Write a macaronic story below on the spaces provided. Be sure to use at least five Latin words. Focus on the words from this week's list by writing a story about animals that escape from the Coliseum. Underline the Latin words you use.

# Review of Lists 1-9: Giant Crossword Puzzle

Fill in the Latin translations of the English words by following the ACROSS and DOWN clues. Match the number of the clue to the numbered boxes going in that direction.

ACROSS
3 boy student _____
4 book _____
5 field _____
8 male friend _____
10 rooster _____
11 olive oil _____
12 brother _____
14 doctor _____
15 gift _____
17 female pig _____
20 game _____
22 building _____
23 female teacher _____

DOWN
1 tongue _____
2 church _____
5 year _____
6 street, road _____
7 hay _____
9 garden _____
13 party _____
14 sickness _____
16 because _____
18 water _____
19 cow _____
21 city _____

Activity Pages 329

A. Review of Lists 9-16: Name What You See

Here is scene filled with things you have studied in Latin. Color and label in Latin the items that are vocabulary words from lists 9-16. Try to do it without looking back at the lists. You may be surprised by how much you know!

Activity Pages

Review of Lists 19-24: Word Search

Search the grid and circle the **Latin translation** of the English words. Words may be spelled forwards, backwards, upwards, downwards, or diagonally.

```
V J L H Y K W T A A N L W L R P
C T A D L P Q G M C R U S R R R
A W N R M Y I I R Q M A R B M U
R Y O L S R M M W H T P A Y R X
B W S D U C A T P M Z E L R M T
U T R A R L L H J E N N T N M V
N Y E V T H O L K A R A T N E F
C K P C I G I R R N L A G N K T
U F N M N L T A L E C A T L C K
L H C K O A S C C R A U P O A H
U H F Z T D E L Q A S V R I R Y
S R M B M I B K K H B O L J S N
R C N R Q U Q T T K N D K I F P
Q F W W D S T Z X A Q G G Q P S M
R T X D L O S A S P E R K Z L B
B N C U R R I C U L U M N M G B
```

insect _____
spider _____
rough, uneven _____
commander _____
sword _____
wind _____
shadow, shade _____
seaweed _____
mask _____
actress _____

leg _____
stone, rock _____
ruby _____
crown _____
sun _____
forest _____
beach, sand _____
charioteer _____
race _____
thunder _____

Activity Pages 331

A Story Illustration

Illustrate the story of the "Billy Goats Gruff." You do not need to label your drawing.

REFERENCE PAGES

A Note About Chants

Learn all the chants in the order they appear on the page – starting with the far left column and moving down the page; then back to the top of the second column, and so forth. Some of the chants are from Logos Latin 1 and some will be explained in Logos Latin 3.

Remember that classical education follows the Trivium and this is a grammar level curriculum. In the grammar stage students memorize and chant many things that they might not understand completely, but as they progress through the Logos Latin series they will build on this knowledge.

Verb Chants

FIRST CONJUGATION

amō	amāmus
amās	amātis
amat	amant

SECOND CONJUGATION

videō	vidēmus
vidēs	vidētis
videt	vident

THIRD CONJUGATION

dūcō	dūcimus
dūcis	dūcitis
dūcit	dūcunt

FOURTH CONJUGATION

audiō	audīmus
audīs	audītis
audit	audiunt

LINKING VERB (PRESENT TENSE)

sum	sumus
es	estis
est	sunt

POSSUM CHANT

possum	possumus
potes	potestis
potest	possunt

PRESENT TENSE VERB ENDINGS

-ō	-mus
-s	-tis
-t	-nt

FUTURE TENSE VERB ENDINGS

-bō	-bimus
-bis	-bitis
-bit	-bunt

IMPERFECT TENSE VERB ENDINGS

-bam	-bāmus
-bās	-bātis
-bat	-bant

PERFECT TENSE VERB ENDINGS

-ī	-imus
-istī	-istis
-it	-ērunt

FUTURE PERFECT TENSE VERB ENDINGS

-erō	-erimus
-eris	-eritis
-erit	-erint

PLUPERFECT TENSE VERB ENDINGS

-eram	-erāmus
-erās	-erātis
-erat	-erant

Reference Pages

R Verb Chants (Continued)

PRESENT PASSIVE VERB ENDINGS

-r	-mur
-ris	-minī
-tur	-ntur

FUTURE PASSIVE VERB ENDINGS

-bor	-bimur
-beris	-biminī
-bitur	-buntur

IMPERFECT PASSIVE VERB ENDINGS

-bar	-bamur
-baris	-baminī
-batur	-bantur

R Noun Chants

Noun chant endings do not have meanings in the same way that verb endings do. Instead, noun endings can tell what part of speech a word is, such as the subject noun. Like verbs, nouns have different families which are called *declensions*.

FIRST DECLENSION

-a	-ae
-ae	-ārum
-ae	-īs
-am	-ās
-ā	-īs

SECOND DECLENSION

-us	-ī
-ī	-ōrum
-ō	-īs
-um	-ōs
-ō	-īs

SECOND DECLENSION NEUTER

-um	-a
-ī	-ōrum
-ō	-īs
-um	-a
-ō	-īs

THIRD DECLENSION

-x	-ēs
-is	-um
-ī	-ibus
-em	-ēs
-e	-ibus

THIRD DECLENSION - I STEM

-is	-ēs
-is	-ium
-ī	-ibus
-em	-ēs
-e	-ibus

THIRD DECLENSION NEUTER

-x	-a
-is	-um
-ī	-ibus
-x	-a
-e	-ibus

Noun Chants (Continued)

FOURTH DECLENSION

-us	-ūs
-ūs	-uum
-uī	-ibus
-um	-ūs
-ū	-ibus

FOURTH DECLENSION NEUTER

-ū	-ua
-ūs	-uum
-ū	-ibus
-ū	-ua
-ū	-ibus

FIFTH DECLENSION

-ēs	-ēs
-ēī	-ērum
-ēi	-ēbus
-em	-ēs
-ē	-ēbus

Pronoun Chants

DEMONSTRATIVE PRONOUNS (memorize these two charts across, not down)

SINGULAR - THIS

→ → →

hic	haec	hoc
huius	huius	huius
huic	huic	huic
hunc	hanc	hoc
hōc	hāc	hōc

PLURAL - THESE

→ → →

hī	hae	haec
hōrum	hārum	hōrum
hīs	hīs	hīs
hōs	hās	haec
hīs	hīs	hīs

PERSONAL PRONOUNS

1. SINGULAR - FIRST PERSON (I/ME)

ego
meī
mihi
mē
mē

3. PLURAL - FIRST PERSON (WE)

nōs
nostrum
nōbis
nōs
nōbīs

2. SINGULAR - SECOND PERSON (YOU)

tū
tuī
tibi
tē
tē

4. PLURAL - SECOND PERSON (YOU ALL)

vōs
vestrum
vōbīs
vōs
vōbīs

Jingles and Nifty Sayings

Five Noun Cases

Nominative → NO

Genitive → GENTLE

Dative → DAD

Accusative → ACCUSES

Ablative → APPLES

How to Find the Noun Base

Don't try to change the case

until you find the base.

The genitive case

is the place to find the base.

LATIN ACTIVE VERB TENSE CHART I

Present (am, is, are, do, does)

Person	Singular	Plural
1st	**ō** I am	**mus** we are
2nd	**s** you are	**tis** you all are
3rd	**t** he, she, it is	**nt** they are

Imperfect (was, were, used to)

Person	Singular	Plural
1st	**bam** I was	**bāmus** we were
2nd	**bās** you were	**bātis** you all were
3rd	**bat** he, she, it was	**bant** they were

Future (will, shall)

Person	Singular	Plural
1st	**bō** I will	**bimus** we will
2nd	**bis** you will	**bitis** you all will
3rd	**bit** he, she, it will	**bunt** they will

Latin Ending Charts

LATIN NOUN ENDINGS CHART I

CASE KEY — **NOM:** NOMINATIVE — **GEN:** GENITIVE — **DAT:** DATIVE — **ACC:** ACCUSATIVE — **ABL:** ABLATIVE

1st Declension

Case	Singular	Plural
Nom	a	ae
Gen	ae	ārum
Dat	ae	īs
Acc	am	ās
Abl	ā	īs

2nd Declension

Case	Singular	Plural
Nom	us	ī
Gen	ī	ōrum
Dat	ō	īs
Acc	um	ōs
Abl	ō	īs

2nd Declension Neuter

Case	Singular	Plural
Nom	um	a
Gen	ī	ōrum
Dat	ō	īs
Acc	um	a
Abl	ō	īs

3rd Declension

Case	Singular	Plural
Nom	x	ēs
Gen	is	um
Dat	ī	ibus
Acc	em	ēs
Abl	e	ibus

3rd Declension Neuter

Case	Singular	Plural
Nom	x	a
Gen	is	um
Dat	ī	ibus
Acc	x	a
Abl	e	ibus

Latin Ending Charts

Memory Work: Psalm 23

Canticum David

1 Dominus pascit mē nihil mihi dēerit

2 in pascuīs herbārum adclīnāvit mē super aquās refectionīs ēnūtrīvit mē

3 animam meam refēcit dūxit mē per sēmitās iūstitiae propter nōmen suum

4 sed et sī ambulāverō in valle mortis nōn timēbō malum quoniam tū mēcum es virga tua et baculum tuum ipsa consōlābuntur mē

5 ponēs cōram mē mensam ex adversō hostium meōrum inpinguāsti oleō caput meum calix meus inēbriāns

6 sed et benīgnitas et misericordia subsequētur mē omnibus diēbus vītae meae et habitābō in domō Dominī in longitūdine diērum

A Psalm of David

1 The Lord is my shepherd; I shall not want

2 He maketh me to lie down in green pastures; He leads me beside the still waters.

3 He restoreth my soul: He leadeth me in the paths of righteousness for His name's sake.

4 Yea, though I walk through the valley of the shadow of death, I will fear no evil: for Thou art with me; Thy rod and Thy staff they comfort me.

5 Thou preparest a table before me in the present of mine enemies; Thou anointest my head with oil; my cup runneth over.

6 Surely goodness and mercy shall follow me all the days of my life: and I will dwell in the house of the Lord for ever.

Memory Work: The Lord's Prayer

Pater Noster

1 Pater noster, quī es in caelīs,
2 sanctificētur nōmen Tuum.
3 Adveniat regnum Tuum;
4 Fiat voluntas Tua
5 sīcut in caelō et in terrā.
6 Pānem nostrum cotīdiānum dā nōbīs hodiē,
7 et dimitte nōbīs dēbita nostra,
8 Sīcut et nōs dimittimus dēbitoribus nostrīs,
9 et ne nōs inducās in tentātiōnem,
10 sed līberā nōs a malō.
11 Āmēn.

The Lord's Prayer

1 Our Father who art in heaven,
2 hallowed be Thy name.
3 Thy kingdom come.
4 Thy will be done
5 on earth as it is in heaven.
6 Give us this day our daily bread,
7 and forgive us our trespasses,
8 as we forgive those who trespass against us,
9 and lead us not into temptation,
10 but deliver us from evil.
11 Amen.

[*The Vulgate omits "For thine is the kingdom, and the power, and the glory, for ever and ever."*]

 Visual Aid: Flower - Verb Stem

(From Lesson 9)

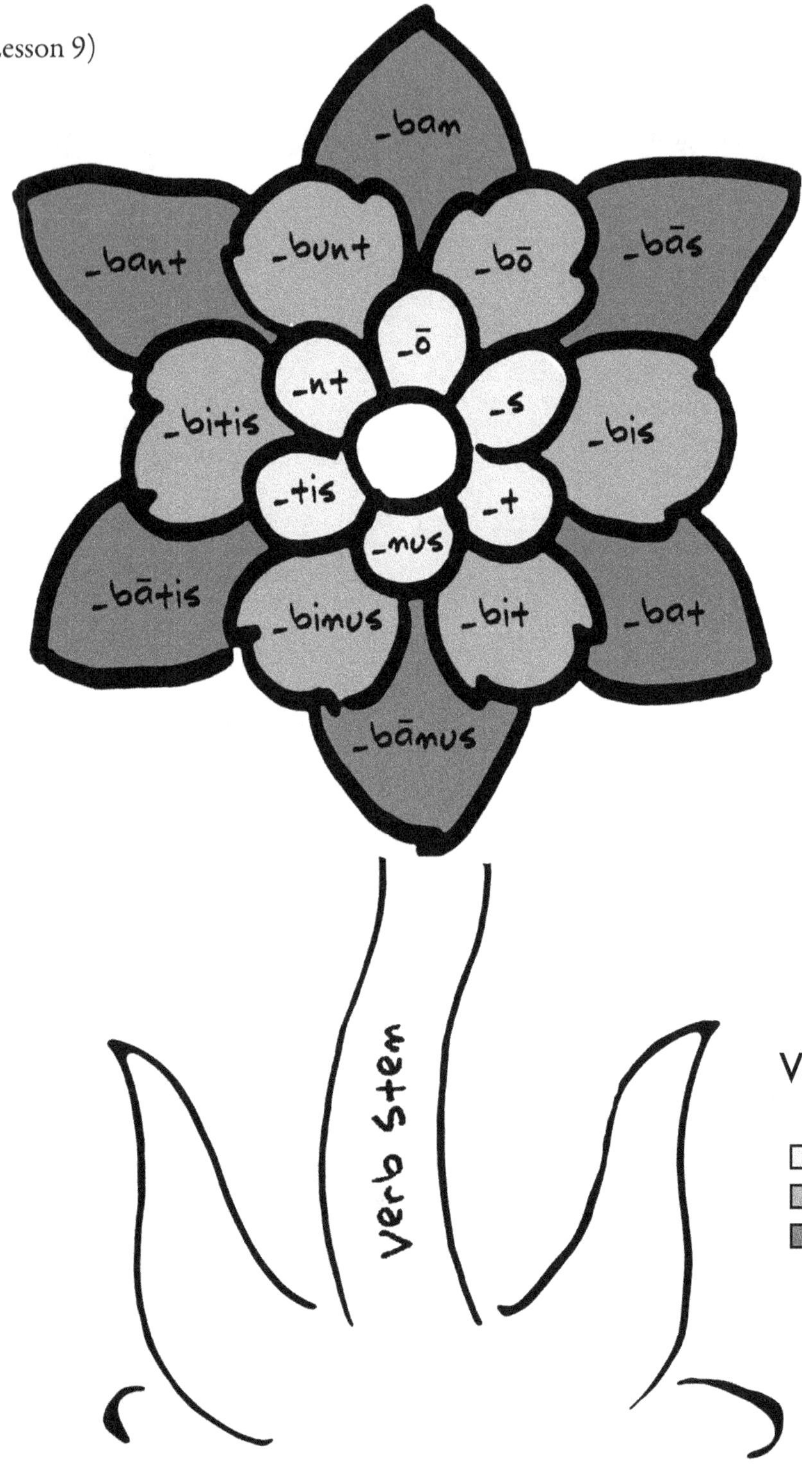

Verb Stem Key

- ☐ Past Tense
- ☐ Future Tense
- ☐ Imperfect Tense

346 Reference Pages

 Visual Aid: "In a Nutshell" – Verb Endings & Meanings

(From Lesson 12)

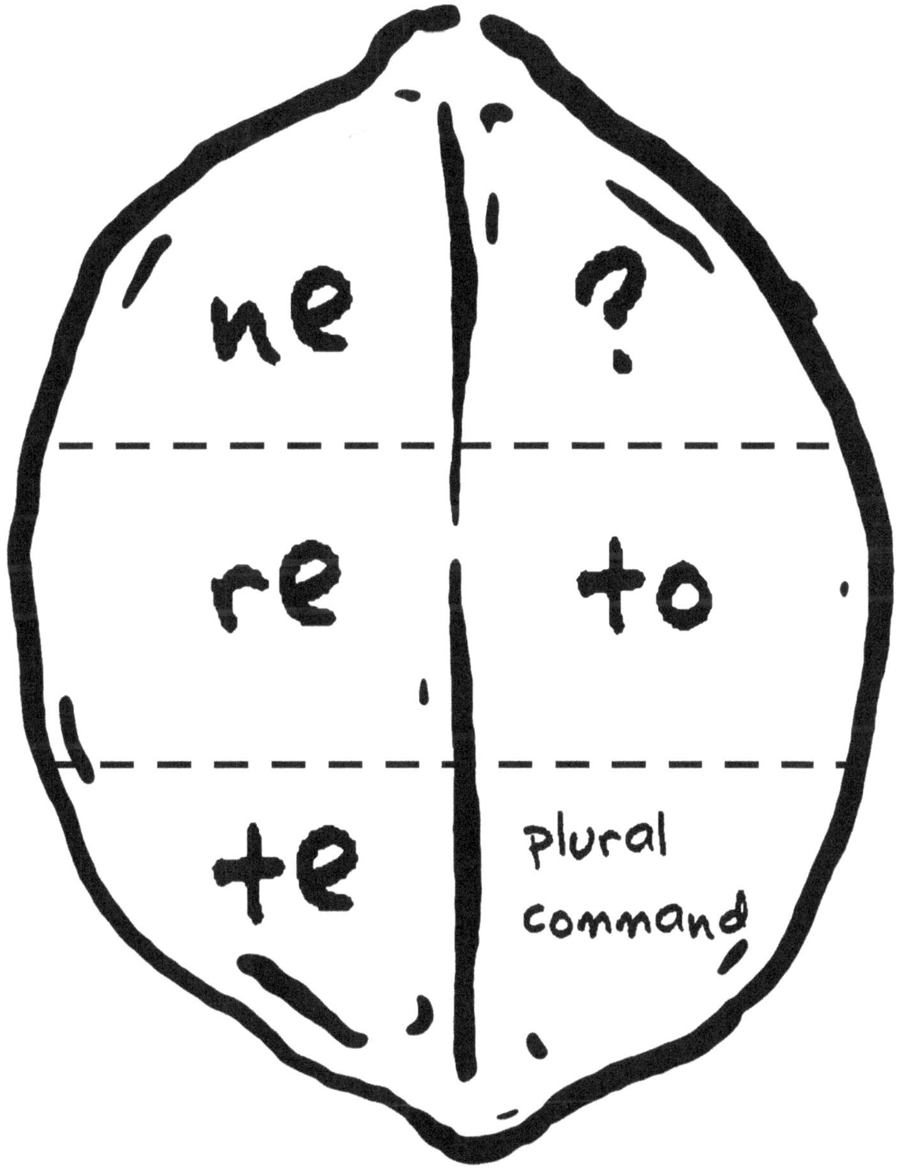

ne	?
re	to
te	plural command

Reference Pages 347

Glossary: Latin to English

The number in parentheses indicates the list in which the word is introduced. Some words from Logos Latin 1 appear only in Review Lists. These words are indicated by the abbreviation *Rv.*.

A

a, ab, *prep. w/ abl.*, from, away (16)
accūrātus,-a,-um, *adj.*, careful, exact (14)
actor, actōris, *m., noun*, actor (24)
acūtus, -a, -um, *adj.*, sharp (11)
ad (+acc), *prep.*, to, toward (3)
adamas, adamantis, *m., noun*, diamond (20)
adiūdicō, adiūdicāre, *verb*, to award (13)
administrō, administrāre, *verb*, to help, assist (11)
aedificium,-i, *n., noun*, building (7)
aedificō, aedificāre, *verb*, to build (23)
aeger, aegra, aegrum, *adj.*, sick (8)
aegrōtō, aegrōtāre, *verb*, to be sick (9)
ager, agri, *m., noun*, field (5)
agnus, -i, *m., noun*, lamb (5)
agricola, -ae, *f., noun*, farmer (Rv. 4)
albus, -a, -um, *adj.*, white (10)
alga, -ae, *f., noun*, seaweed (23)
altus, -a, -um, *adj.*, high, tall (12)
ambulō, ambulāre, *verb*, to walk (3)
amīca, -ae, *m., noun*, female friend (2)
amīcus, -ī, *m., noun*, male friend (2)
ampulla, -ae, *f., noun*, flask, bottle (6)
ancilla, -ae, *f., noun*, maidservant (3)
animōsus, -a,-um, *adj.*, courageous (14)
annus, -ī, *m., noun*, year (8)
anulus, -ī, *m., noun*, ring (11)

apportō, apportāre, *verb*, to bring (3)
aqua, -ae, *f., noun*, water (5)
arānea, -ae, *f., noun*, spider (19)
arbor, arboris, *f., noun*, tree (Rv. 19)
argentāria,-ae, *f., noun*, bank (7)
argentum, -ī, *n., noun*, silver, money (13)
arithmētica, -ae, *f., noun*, arithmetic (1)
armilla, -ae, *f., noun*, bracelet (11)
arō, arāre, *verb*, to plow (5)
asper, aspera, asperum, *adj.*, rough, uneven (20)
astō, astāre, *verb*, to stand near (14)
audiō, *verb* (to) hear (p. 90)
**aurīga, -ae, m.* or *f.*, *noun*, charioteer (24)
aurum, -ī, *n., noun*, gold (11)
auscultō, auscultāre, *verb*, to listen to (Rv. 21)
avārus,-a,-um, *adj.*, greedy (17)
avia, -ae, *f., noun*, grandmother (Rv. 4)
avūnculus, -ī, *m., noun*, uncle (18)
avus, -ī, *m., noun*, grandfather (Rv. 4)

B

bacca, -ae, *noun*, berry (6)
basilica, -ae, *f., noun*, court building (18)
bene, *adv.*, well (15)
bestia serpens, *f., phrase*, reptile (19)
bestiola, -ae, *f., noun*, insect (19)
bonus, -a, um, *adj.*, good, Rv. (18)

C

caeruleus, -a, -um, *adj.*, blue (10)
calceus, -ī, *m., noun*, shoe (10)

calcitrō, calcitrāre, *verb*, to kick (12)
campus, -ī, *m., noun*, athletic field (12)
candēla, -ae, *f., noun*, candle (8)
canis, canis, *m. or f., noun*, dog (16)
canō, canāre, *verb*, to crow (4)
cantō, cantāre, *verb*, to sing (Rv. 8)
capra, -ae, *f., noun*, female goat (4)
carbunculus, -ī, *m., noun*, ruby (20)
carcer, carceris, *m., noun*, prison (17)
carmen, carminis, *n., noun*, song (21)
caseus, -ī, *m., noun*, cheese (22)
castellum, -ī, *n., noun*, castle (23)
cavum, -ī, *n., noun*, hole (6)
celebrō, celebrāre, *verb*, to celebrate (8)
cēna, -ae, *f., noun*, dinner, meal (3)
charta, -ae, *f., noun*, piece of paper (Rv. 2)
cicāda, -ae, *f., noun*, tree cricket (19)
circus,- i, *m., noun*, race course (24)
citus, -a, -um, *adj.*, fast, swift (12)
cīvis, cīvis, *m. or f., noun*, citizen (17)
clāmō, clamāre, *verb*, to shout (12)
columna,-ae, *f., noun*, column (7)
coma, -ae, *f., noun*, hair, leaves (10)
commūnicō, commūnicāre, *verb*, to share (22)
compleō, complēre, *verb*, to fill up (6)
comportō, comportāre, *verb*, to collect (16)
consul, consulis, *m., noun*, consul (18)
convīvium, -ī, *n, noun*, party (8)
corōna, -ae, *f., noun*, crown (21)
crās, *adv.*, tomorrow (14)
creō, creāre, *verb*, make, create (18)
crūs, crūris, *n., noun*, leg (19)
cubō, cubāre, *verb*, to lie down (9)
cum (+abl), *prep.*, with (6)

cūria, -ae, *f., noun*, senate building (18)
curō, curāre, *verb*, to care for (5)
curriculum, -ī, *n., noun*, race (24)

D

damnō, damnāre, *verb*, to condemn (17)
decem, *adj.*, ten (Rv. 8)
decimus, -a, -um, *adj.*, tenth (13)
dēvorō, dēvorāre, *verb*, to swallow (9)
diēs natālis, *phrase*, birthday (8)
discipula, -ae, *f., noun*, girl student (1)
discipulus, -ī, *m., noun*, boy student (1)
disputō, disputāre, *verb*, to discuss, argue (18)
diū, *adv.*, for a long time (15)
dō, dāre, *verb*, to give (4)
doleō, dolēre, *verb*, to grieve (9)
dolor stomachī, *phrase*, stomach ache (9)
dominus, -ī, *m., noun*, lord, master (Rv. 4)
dōmus, -ūs, *f., noun*, home (Rv. 16)
dōnum, -ī, *n., noun*, gift (8)
dūcō, *verb*, to lead (p. 74)
duo, *adj.*, two (Rv. 8)
dūrus, -a, -um, *adj.*, hard (20)

E

ecclēsia,-ae, *f., noun*, church (7)
elephāntus, -ī, *m., noun*, elephant (24)
eques, equites, *m., noun*, knight (21)
equitō, equitāre, *verb*, to ride on horseback (Rv. 4)
equus, -ī, *m., noun*, horse (Rv. 12)
errō, errāre, *verb*, to wander, err (7)
est, *verb*, is (Rv. 3)
et, *conj.*, and (Rv. 1)
exclāmō, exclāmāre, *verb*, to exclaim (7)
explōrō, explōrāre, *verb*, to explore (14)
exspectō, exspecto, *verb*, to wait for (14)
exspoliō, exspoliāre, *verb*, to rob (16)

F
fābula, -ae, *f., noun,* story (2)
faenum, -i, *n., noun,* hay (4)
fēles, fēlis, *f., noun,* cat (16)
femina, -ae, *f. noun,* woman (Rv. 24)
fenestra, -ae, *f., noun,* window (12)
ferus, -ī, *m., noun,* wild animal (14)
fīlia regis, f., *f., phrase,* princess (21)
fīlia sorōris, *phrase,* niece (18)
fīlius sorōris, *phrase,* nephew (18)
firmō, firmāre, *verb,* to strengthen (15)
flāvus, -a, -um, *adj.,* yellow, blond (10)
flō, flāre, *verb,* to blow (8)
floreō, florēre, *verb,* to bloom, flourish (6)
flūtō, flūtāre, *verb,* to float (23)
fluvius, -ī, *m., noun,* river (15)
focus, -ī, *m., noun,* hearth, fireplace (3)
fodicō, fodicāre, *verb,* to dig (6)
foedus, -a, -um, *adj.,* ugly (11)
folium, -ī, *n., noun,* leaf (Rv. 19)
forum, -i, *n., noun,* public square (7)
frāter, fratris, *m., noun,* brother (3)
frustum, -ī, *n., noun,* piece (9)
frutex, fruticis, *m., noun,* bush (16)
fugitō, fugitāre, *verb,* to flee from (14)
fulvus, -a, -um, *adj.,* brown (10)
fūmus, -ī, *m., noun,* smoke (8)
furtim, *adv.,* stealthily (16)

G
gallina, -ae, *f., noun,* hen (Rv. 4)
gallus, -i, *m., noun,* rooster (4)
gāvia, -ae, *f., noun,* seagull (23)
gemma, -ae, *f., noun,* jewel (11)
geōgraphia, -ae, *f., noun,* geography (2)
gestō, gestāre, *verb,* to wear (24)
gladiātor, gladiātōris, *m., noun,* gladiator (21)

gladius, -ī, *m., noun,* sword (21)
globulus, -ī, *m., noun,* button (Rv. 10)
grāmen, grāminis, *n., noun,* grass (19)
gryllus, -ī, *m., noun,* grasshopper (19)
gubernō, gubernāre, *noun,* govern, steer (18)

H
habeō, habēre, *verb,* to have, hold (2)
harena, -ae, *f., noun,* beach, sand (23)
herba, -ae, *f., noun,* plant (Rv. 6)
herbācea, -a, -um, *adj.,* olive green (p125)
herī, *adv.,* yesterday (14)
hippocampus, -ī, *m., noun,* seahorse (23)
historia, -ae, *f., noun,* history (1)
hodiē, *adv.,* today (14)
horreum, -ī, *n., noun,* barn (4)
hortus, -ī, *m., noun,* garden (6)

I
iactō, iactāre, *verb,* to throw (12)
iānitor, ianitoris, *m., noun,* doorkeeper (18)
iānua, -ae, *f., noun,* door (18)
imperātor, imperātōris, *m., noun,* commander (21)
imperō, imperāre, *verb,* to order (17)
in (+abl), *prep.,* in, on (3)
in (+acc), *prep.,* into (3)
īnfāns, īnfāntis, *m., noun,* infant (Rv. 24)
inlaqueō, inlaqueāre, *verb,* to entrap (16)
inter (+acc), *prep.,* between, among (19)
intrō, intrāre, *verb,* to enter (18)
invītō, invītāre, *verb,* to invite (3)
īrātus, -a, -um, *adj.,* angry (12)
iūdex, iūdicis, *m., noun,* judge, juror (17)
iūdicium, -ī, *n., noun,* trial, court (17)
iuvō, iuvāre, *verb,* to help (5)
labōrō, labōrāre, *verb,* to work (5)

L
lacerta, -ae, *f., noun,* lizard (19)

lāna, -ae, *f., noun,* wool (5)
lapicīdīnae, -arum, *f., noun,* rock quarry (20)
lapidō, lapidāre, *verb,* to throw stones at (20)
lapidōsus, -a, -um, *adj.,* stony (20)
lapis, lapidis, *m., noun,* stone, rock (20)
lapsō, lapsāre, *verb,* to slip, stumble (20)
later, lateris, *m., noun,* brick (20)
lātrō, latrāre, *verb,* to bark (at) (16)
lātus, -a, -um, *adj.,* wide (12)
laurea, -ae, *f., noun,* laurel wreath (13)
lectus, -i, *m., noun,* bed (9)
leo, leōnis, *m., noun,* lion (24)
levō, levāre, *verb,* to lift up (20)
lex, legis, *f., noun,* law (16)
liber, libri, *m., noun,* book (1)
līberī, līberōrum, *m., noun,* children (Rv. 20)
libō, libāre, *verb,* to taste (Rv. 4)
lībum natāle, *phrase,* birthday cake (8)
lignum, -ī, *n., noun,* log (15)
limbus, -ī, *m., noun,* border, hem (18)
līmo, līmāre, *verb,* to polish (11)
lingua, -ae, *f., noun,* tongue (9)
littera, -ae, *f., noun,* letter (1)
longus, -a, -um, , *adj.,* long (11)
lūceō, lūcēre, *verb,* to shine, be bright (22)
lūcus, -ī, *m., noun,* grove (6)
lūdus scaenicus,, *phrase,* a play (24)
lūdus, -ī, *m., noun,* school, game (2)
lutum, -ī, *n., noun,* mud (22)

M magister, magistrī, *m., noun,* male teacher (1)
magistra, -ae, *f., noun,* female teacher (1)
magnus, -a, -um, *adj.,* large (10)
mālum, -ī, *n., noun,* apple (Rv. 4)
mandūcō, mandūcāre, *verb,* to chew, eat (19)

mannulus,-i, *m., noun,* pony (4)
mappa, -ae, *f., noun,* napkin (8)
margarīta, -ae, *f., noun,* pearl (11)
māter, mātris, *f., noun,* mother (3)
medicāmentum, -ī, *n., noun,* medicine (9)
medicus, -ī, *m., noun,* doctor (9)
mensa secūnda, *f., phrase,* dessert (22)
mensa, -ae, *f., noun,* desk, table (2)
mīles, mīlitis, *m., noun,* soldier (17)
mīma, -ae, *f., noun,* actress (24)
moneō, monēre, *verb,* to warn (9)
monstrō, monstrāre, *verb,* point out (2)
monumentum,-ī, *n., noun,* monument (7)
morbus, -ī, *m., m., noun,* sickness (9)
moveo, -ere, *verb,* move (Rv. 12)
mulgeō, mulgēre, *verb,* to milk (5)
mūrus, -ī, *m., noun,* wall (12)
muscōsus, -a, -um, *adj.,* mossy (15)
mūsica, -ae, *f., noun,* music (21)

N narrō, narrāre, *verb,* to tell, say (Rv. 9)
neō, nēre, *verb,* to spin, weave (19)
niger, nigra, nigrum, *adj.,* black (10)
nō, nāre, *verb,* to swim (15)
nōn, *adv.,* not (Rv. 4)
nōnus, -a, -um, *adj.,* ninth (13)
notā bene, *phrase,* note well (Rv. 1)
novem, *adj.,* nine (Rv. 8)
nox, noctis, *f., noun,* night (16)
numerō, numerāre, *verb,* to count (2)
numerus, -ī, *m., noun,* number (2)
nunc, *adv.,* now (15)
nuntiō, nuntiāre, *verb,* to announce (13)

O occultō, occultāre, *verb,* to hide (8)
ōceanus, -ī, *m., noun,* ocean (23)

octāvus, -a, -um, *adj.,* eighth (13)
octo, *adj.,* eight (Rv. 8)
oleum, -ī, *n., noun,* olive oil (6)
olīva, -ae, *f., noun,* olive, olive tree (6)
ōra marītima, *f., phrase,* seashore (23)
ōrātio, ōrātiōnis, *f., noun,* speech (21)
ōrātor, ōrātōris, *m., noun,* speaker (21)
ornō, ornāre, *verb,* to decorate, equip (8)
ostendē, *verb (imp.),* stick out (9)
ovis, ovis, *f., noun,* sheep (5)
ovum, -ī, *n., noun,* egg (Rv. 4)

P

pala, -ae, *f., noun,* shovel (Rv. 6)
palla, -ae, *f., noun,* cloak (10)
parens, parentis, *m. or f., noun,* parent (16)
pareō parēre, *verb,* to obey (16)
parō, parāre, *verb,* to prepare (3)
parvus, -a, -um, *adj.,* small, little (10)
pastor, pastōris, *m., noun,* shepherd (Rv. 5)
pater, patris, *m., noun,* father (3)
pecunia, -ae, *f., noun,* money (Rv. 12)
per (+acc), *prep.,* through (12 & 22)
persōna, -ae, *f., noun,* mask (24)
pila, -ae, *f., noun,* ball (12)
pilula, -ae, *f., noun,* pill (9)
pirum, -ī, *n., noun,* pear (22)
plaustrum, -ī, *n., noun,* cart (12)
plūvia, -ae, *f., noun,* rain (22)
pomarium, -ī, *n., noun,* orchard (Rv. 6)
pompa, -ae, *f., noun,* parade (21)
pōmum, -ī, *n., noun,* fruit (4)
porca, -ae, *f., noun,* female pig (5)
porcellus, - i, *m., noun,* little pig (5)
porcus, -ī, *m., noun,* male pig (5)
portō, portāre, *verb,* to carry (Rv. 7)

possum, posse, *verb,* to be able (4)
pōtō, pōtāre, *verb,* to drink (5)
praedium, -ī, *n., noun,* farm (4)
praedo, praedōnis, *m., noun,* robber (16)
praefectus, -ī, *m., noun,* officer (17)
praemium, -ī, *n., noun,* reward, prize (13)
prandium, -ī, *n., noun,* lunch (22)
prātum,-i, *n., noun,* meadow (4)
prīmus, -a, -um, *adj.,* first (13)
properō, properāre, *verb,* to hurry (Rv. 12)
prōvolō, provolāre, *verb,* to dart, dash (19)
psittacus, -i, *m., noun,* parrot (16)
puer, -ī, *m., noun,* boy (Rv. 7)
pugnō, pugnāre, *verb,* to fight (24)
pulcher, pulchra, pulchrum, *adj.,* beautiful (11)
purpureus,- a, -um, *noun,* purple (18)
putō, putāre, *verb,* to prune (6)

Q

quālus, -ī, *m., noun,* basket (6)
quartus, -a, -um, *adj.,* fourth (13)
quassō, quassāre, *verb,* to break in pieces (20)
quattuor, *adj.,* four (Rv. 8)
Quid est?, *phrase,* What is it? (Rv. 1)
quinque, *adj.,* five (Rv. 8)
quintus, -a, -um, *adj.,* fifth (13)
Quis est?, *phrase,* Who is it? (Rv. 1)
quod, *conj.,* because (9)

R

rāmus, -ī, *m., noun,* branch (6)
recitō, recitāre, *verb,* to recite (1)
redundō, redundāre, *verb,* to overflow (15)
relegō, relegāre, *verb,* to send away (17)
repente, *adv.,* suddenly (15)
respondeō, respondēre, *verb,* to answer (2)
retineō, -ere, *verb (to)* hold back (14)
rēx, rēgis, *m., noun,* king (Rv. 21)

rīdeō, ridēre, *verb,* to laugh, smile (24)
rīpa, -ae, *f., noun,* riverbank (15)
rogō, rogāre, *verb,* to ask (1)
Rōma, -ae, *f., noun,* Rome (7)
roseus, -a, -um, *adj.,* pink (10)
rotundus, -a, -um, *adj.,* round (12)
ruber, rubra, rubrum, *adj.,* red (10)

S

saepe, *adv.,* often (15)
saltātrix, saltātricis, *f., noun,* dancer (21)
saltō, saltāre, *verb,* to dance (8)
salve, *verb (imp.),* hello (Rv. 1)
saxulum, -ī, *n., noun,* little rock (20)
saxum, -ī, *n., noun,* rock (4)
scaena, -ae, *f., noun,* stage (24)
sceleratus, -a, -um, *adj.,* guilty (17)
sceptrum, -i, *n., noun,* scepter (21)
schola, -ae, *f., noun,* class, classroom (Rv. 13)
scūtum, -ī, *n., noun,* shield (11)
secō, secāre, *verb,* to cut (4)
secundus, -a, -um, *adj.,* second (13)
sed, *conj.,* but (Rv. 15)
sedeō, sedēre, *verb,* to sit (Rv. 15)
sella, -ae, *f., noun,* seat, chair (2)
semper, *adv.,* always (15)
senātor, senātōris, *m., noun,* senator (18)
senex, senis, *m., noun,* old man (Rv. 18)
sententia, -ae, *f., noun,* opinion (17)
septem, *adj.,* seven (Rv. 8)
septimus, -a, um, *adj.,* seventh (13)
serpens, serpentis, *m. or f., noun,* snake (19)
servō, servāre, *verb,* to save (15)
servus, -ī, *m., noun,* slave, servant (3)
sex, *adj.,* six (Rv. 8)
sextus, -a, -um, *adj.,* sixth (13)

sībilō, sībilāre, *verb,* to whistle, hiss (at) (16)
sīca, -ae, *f., noun,* dagger (11)
silva, -ae, *f., noun,* forest (22)
simulō, simulāre, *verb,* to pretend (21)
smaragdus, -ī, *m. or f., noun,* emerald (20)
sōl, sōlis, *m., noun,* sun (22)
sonō, sonāre, *verb,* to sound (22)
soror, sorōris, *f., noun,* sister (3)
spectō, spectāre, *verb,* to look at (2)
spēlunca, -ae, *f., noun,* cave (14)
stabulum, -ī, *n., noun,* stall, stable (Rv. 4)
statua, -ae, *f., noun,* statue (7)
stō, stāre, *verb,* to stand (7)
stola, -ae, *f., noun,* dress (10)
stomachus, -ī, *noun, m.,* stomach (8)
struō, struāre, *verb,* to pile up (4)
studeō, studēre, *verb,* to study (2)
stylus, -ī, *m., noun,* pencil (Rv. 2)
sūcus, -ī, *m., noun,* juice (22)

T

taberna, -ae, *f., noun,* shop (Rv. 11)
tabernārius, -ī, *m., noun,* shopkeeper (11)
tabula, -ae, *f., noun,* map, board (2)
tardus, -a, -um, *adj.,* slow (12)
tela, -ae, *f., noun,* web (19)
templum, -i, *n., noun,* temple (7)
terra, -ae, *f., noun,* land (Rv. 12)
tertius, -a, -um, *adj.,* third (13)
testimōnium, -ī, *n., noun,* testimony (17)
testis, testis, *m. or f., noun,* witness (17)
textum, -ī, *n., noun,* cloth (10)
theātrum, -ī, *n., noun,* theater (24)
thermopōlium, -i, *n., noun,* hot food shop (7)
thēsaurus, -ī, *m., noun,* treasure (14)
tigris, tigris, *m., noun,* tiger (24)

Glossary: Latin to English

timidus,-a,-um, *adj.,* fearful (14)
tītillō, tītillāre, *verb,* to tickle (19)
toga, -ae, *f., noun,* toga (10)
tondeō, tondēre, *verb,* to shear, shave, clip (5)
tonitrus, -us, *m., noun,* thunder (22)
trabea, -ae, *f., noun,* robe of state (21)
tractō, tractāre, *verb,* to drag along, haul (20)
trans (+acc), *prep.,* over, across, (23)
tres, *adj.,* three (Rv. 8)
tum, *adv.,* then (15)
tunica, -ae, *f., noun,* tunic (Rv. 10)

U **ululō, ululāre,** *verb,* to howl, scream (Rv. 14)
umbella, -ae, *f., noun,* parasol (23)
umbra, -ae, *f., noun,* shadow, shade (23)
unda, -ae, *f., noun,* wave (23)
unus, -a, -um, *adj.,* one (Rv. 8)
urbs, urbis, *f., noun,* city (7)
ustulō, ustulāre, *verb,* to burn (23)
ūva, -ae, *f., noun,* grape (6)

V **vacca, -ae,** *f., noun,* cow (4)
vale, *verb (imp.),* good bye (Rv. 8)
venditō, venditāre, *verb,* to sell (11)
ventus, -ī, *m., noun,* wind (22)
via,-ae, *f., noun,* street, road, (7)
videō, vidēre, *verb,* to see (Rv. 22)
vigilō, vigilāre, *verb,* to guard (17)
villa, -ae, *f., noun,* farmhouse (Rv. 5)
vinea, -ae, *f., noun,* vineyard (Rv. 6)
vinum, -ī, *n., noun,* wine (Rv. 6)
vir, -ī, *m., noun,* man (Rv. 24)
visitō, visitāre, *verb,* to visit (3)
vocō, vocāre, *verb,* to call (14)
volō, volāre, *verb,* to fly (23)

Glossary: English to Latin

The number in parentheses indicates the list in which the word is introduced. Some words from Logos Latin 1 appear only in Review Lists. These words are indicated by the abbreviation *Rv.*.

A
- (to be) able, *verb,* possum, posse (4)
- actor, *noun,* actor, actōris, *m.* (24)
- actress, *noun,* mīma, -ae, *f.* (24)
- always, *adv.,* semper (15)
- and, *conj.,* et (Rv. 1)
- angry, *adj.,* īrātus, -a, -um (12)
- animal, wild, *noun,* ferus, -ī, *m.* (14)
- (to) announce, *verb,* nuntiō, nuntiāre (13)
- (to) answer, *verb,* respondeō, respondēre (2)
- apple, *noun,* mālum, -ī, *n.* (Rv. 4)
- arithmetic, *noun,* arithmētica, -ae, *f.* (1)
- (to) ask, *verb,* rogō, rogāre (1)
- athletic field, *noun,* campus, -ī, *m,* (12)
- (to) award, *verb,* adiūdicō, adiūdicāre (13)

B
- ball, *noun,* pila, -ae, *f.* (12)
- bank, *noun,* argentāria,-ae, *f.* (7)
- (to) bark (at), *verb,* lātrō, latrāre (16)
- barn, *noun,* horreum, -ī, *n.* (4)
- basket, *noun,* quālus, -ī, *m.* (6)
- beach, sand, *noun,* harena, -ae, *f.* (23)
- beautiful, *adj.,* pulcher, pulchra, pulchrum (11)
- because, *conj.,* quod (9)
- bed, *noun,* lectus, -i, *m.* (9)
- berry, *noun,* bacca, -ae, *f.* (6)
- between, among, *prep.,* inter (+acc) (19)
- birthday, *phrase,* diēs natālis (8)
- birthday cake, *phrase,* lībum natāle (8)
- black, *adj.,* niger, nigra, nigrum (10)
- blond, yellow, *adj.,* flavus, -a, -um (10)
- (to) bloom, flourish, *verb,* floreō, florēre (6)
- (to) blow, *verb,* flō, flāre (8)
- blue, *adj.,* caeruleus, -a, -um (10)
- book, *noun,* liber, libri, *m.* (1)
- border, hem, *noun,* limbus, -ī, *m.* (18)
- boy, *noun,* puer, -ī, *m.* (Rv. 7)
- boy student, *noun,* discipulus, -ī, *m.* (1)
- bracelet, *noun,* armilla, -ae, *f.* (11)
- branch, *noun,* rāmus, -ī, *m.* (6)
- (to) break in pieces, *verb,* quassō, quassāre (20)
- brick, *noun,* later, lateris, *m.* (20)
- (to be) bright, shine, *verb,* luceō, lucēre, (22)
- (to) bring, *verb,* apportō, apportāre, (3)
- brother, *noun,* frāter, fratris, *m.* (3)
- brown, *adj.,* fulvus, -a, -um (10)
- (to) build, *verb,* aedificō, aedificāre (23)
- building, *noun,* aedificium,-i, *n.* (7)
- (to) burn, *verb,* ustulō, ustulāre (23)
- bush, *noun,* frutex, fruticis, *m.* (16)
- but, *conj.,* sed (Rv. 15)
- button, *noun,* globulus, -ī, *m.* (Rv. 10)

C
- (to) call, *verb,* vocō, vocāre (14)
- candle, *noun,* candēla, -ae, *f.* (8)
- (to) care for, *verb,* curō, curāre (5)
- careful, exact, *adj..,* accūrātus,-a,-um (14)

(to) carry, *verb,* portō, portāre (Rv. 7)
cart, wagon, *noun,* plaustrum, -ī, *n.* (12)
castle, *noun,* castellum, -ī, *n.* (23)
cat, *noun,* fēles, fēlis, *f.* (16)
cave, *noun,* spēlunca, -ae, *f.* (14)
(to) celebrate, *verb,* celebrō, celebrāre (8)
charioteer, *noun,* aurīga, -ae, *m.* or *f.* (24)
cheese, *noun,* caseus, -ī, *m.,* (22)
(to) chew, eat, *verb,* mandūcō, mandūcāre (19)
children, *noun,* līberī, līberōrum, *m.* (Rv. 20)
church, *noun,* ecclēsia,-ae, *f.* (7)
citizen, *noun,* cīvis, cīvis, *m.* or *f.* (17)
city, *noun,* urbs, urbis (7)
class, classroom, *noun,* schola, -ae, *f.* (Rv. 13)
cloak, *noun,* palla, -ae, *f.* (10)
cloth, *noun,* textum, -ī, *m.* (10)
(to) collect, *verb,* comportō, comportāre (16)
column, *noun,* columna,-ae, *f.* (7)
commander, *noun,* imperātor, imperātōris, *m.* (21)
(to) condemn, *verb,* damnō, damnāre, (17)
consul, *noun,* consul, consulis, *m.* (18)
(to) copy, pretend, *verb,* simulō, simulāre (Rv. 21)
(to) count, *verb,* numerō, numerāre (2)
courageous, *adj.,* animōsus, -a,-um (14)
court, trial, *noun,* iūdicium, -ī, *n.* (17)
court building, *noun,* basilica, -ae, *f.* (18)
cow, *noun,* vacca, -ae, *f.* (4)
(to) create, make, *verb,* creō, creāre (18)
(to) crow, *verb,* canō, canāre (4)
crown, *noun,* corōna, -ae, *f.* (21)
(to) cut, *verb,* secō, secāre (4)

D
dagger, *noun,* sīca, -ae, *f.* (11)

(to) dance, *verb,* saltō, saltāre (8)
dancer, *noun,* saltātrix, saltātricis, *f.* (21)
(to) dart, dash, *verb,* prōvolō, provolāre (19)
(to) decorate, equip, *verb,* ornō, ornāre(8)
desk, table, *noun,* mensa, -ae, *f.* (2)
dessert, *phrase,* mensa secūnda, *f.,* (22)
diamond, *noun,* adamas, adamantis, *m.* (20)
(to) dig, *verb,* fodicō, fodicāre (6)
dinner, meal, *noun,* cēna, -ae, *f.* (3)
(to) discuss, argue, *verb,* disputō, disputāre (18)
doctor, *noun,* medicus, -ī, *m.* (9)
dog, *noun,* canis, canis , *m.* or *f.* (16)
door, *noun,* iānua, -ae, *f.* (18)
doorkeeper, *noun,* iānitor, ianitoris, *m.* (18)
(to) drag along, haul, *verb,* tractō, tractāre (20)
dress, *noun,* stola, -ae, *f.* (10)
(to) drink, *verb,* pōtō, pōtāre (5)

E
egg, *noun,* ovum, -ī, *n.* (Rv. 4)
eight, *adj.,* octo (Rv. 8)
eighth, *adj.,* octāvus, -a, -um (13)
elephant, *noun,* elephāntus, -ī, *m.* (24)
emerald, *noun,* smaragdus, -i , *m.* or *f.* (20)
(to) enter, *verb,* intrō, intrāre (18)
(to) entrap, *verb,* inlaqueō, inlaqueāre (16)
(to) err, wander, *verb,* errō, errāre (7)
exact, careful, *adj.,* accūrātus,-a,-um (14)
(to) exclaim, *verb,* exclāmō, exclāmāre (7)
(to) explore, *verb,* explōrō, explōrāre (14)

F
farm, *noun,* praedium, -ī, *n.* (4)
farmer, *noun,* agricola, -ae, *m.* (Rv. 4)
farmhouse, *noun,* villa, -ae, *f.* (Rv. 5)
fast, swift, *adj.,* citus, -a, -um (12)
father, *noun,* pater, patris, *m.* (3)
fearful, *adj.,* timidus,-a,-um (14)

Glossary: English to Latin

female friend, *noun,* amīca, -ae, *m.* (2)
female goat, *noun,* capra, -ae, *f.,* (4)
female pig, *noun,* porca, -ae, *f.* (5)
female teacher, *noun,* magistra, -ae, *f.* (1)
field, *noun,* ager, agri, *m.* (5)
fifth, *adj.,* quintus, -a, -um (13)
(to) fight, *verb,* pugnō, pugnāre (24)
(to) fill up, *verb,* compleō, complēre (6)
fireplace, hearth, *noun,* focus, -ī, *m.* (3)
first, *adj.,* prīmus, -a, -um (13)
five, *adj.,* quinque (Rv. 8)
flask, bottle, *noun,* ampulla, -ae, *f.* (6)
(to) flee from, *verb,* fugitō, fugitāre (14)
(to) float, *verb,* flūtō, flūtāre (23)
(to) flourish, bloom, *verb,* floreō, florēre (6)
(to) fly, *verb,* volō, volāre (23)
for a long time, *adv.,* diū (15)
forest, *noun,* silva, -ae, *f.* (22)
four, *adj.,* quattuor, (Rv. 8)
fourth, *adj.,* quartus, -a, -um (13)
friend, female, *noun,* amīca, -ae , *m.* (2)
friend, male , *noun,* amīcus, -ī, *m.* (2)
from, away, *prep. w/ abl.,* a,ab (16)
fruit, *noun,* pōmum, -ī, n. (4)

G

game, school, *noun,* lūdus, -ī, *m.* (2)
garden, *noun,* hortus, -ī, *m.* (6)
geography , *noun,* geōgraphia, -ae, *f.* (2)
gift, *noun,* dōnum, -ī, n. (8)
girl student, *noun,* discipula, -ae, *f.* (1)
(to) give, *verb,* dō, dāre, (4)
gladiator, *noun,* gladiātor, gladiātōris, *m.* (21)
goat, female, *noun,* capra, -ae, *f.* (4)
gold, *noun,* aurum, -ae, *m.* (11)
good, *adj.,* bonus, -a, um (Rv. 18)

good bye, *verb (imp.),* vale (Rv. 8)
(to) govern, steer, *verb,* gubernō, gubernāre (18)
grandfather, *noun,* avus, -ī, *m.* (Rv. 4)
grandmother, *noun,* avia, -ae, *f.* (Rv. 4)
grape, *noun,* ūva, -ae, *f.* (6)
grass, *noun,* grāmen, grāminis, *n.* (19)
grasshopper, *noun,* gryllus, -ī, *m.* (19)
greedy, *adj.,* avārus,-a,-um (17)
(to) grieve, *verb,* doleō, dolēre (9)
grove, *noun,* lūcus, -ī, *m.* (6)
(to) guard, *verb,* vigilō, vigilāre (17)
guilty, *adj.,* sceleratus, -a, -um (17)

H

hair, leaves, *noun,* coma, -ae, *f.* (10)
hard, *adj.,* dūrus, -a, -um (20)
(to) haul, drag along,, *verb,* tractō, tractāre (20)
(to) have, hold, *verb,* habeō, habēre (2)
hay, *noun,* faenum,-i, *n.* (4)
(to) hear, *verb,* aūdiō (p. 90)
hearth, fireplace, *noun,* focus, -ī, *m.* (3)
hello, *verb (imp.),* salve (Rv. 1)
(to) help, *verb,* iuvō, iuvāre, (5)
(to) help, assist, *verb,* administrō, administrāre (11)
hen, *noun,* gallina, -ae, *f.* (Rv. 4)
(to) hide, *verb,* occultō, occultāre (8)
high, tall, *adj.,* altus, -a, -um (12)
(to) hiss, whistle (at), *verb,* sībilō, sībilāre (16)
history, *noun,* historia, -ae, *f.* (1)
(to) hold back, *verb,* retineō, -ere (14)
hole, *noun,* cavum, -ī, *n.* (6)
home, house, *noun,* dōmus, -ūs, *f.* (Rv. 16)
horse, *noun,* equus, -ī, *m.* (Rv. 12)
hot food shop, *noun,* thermopōlium,-i, *n.* (7)

Glossary: English to Latin

I

(to) **howl, scream,** *verb,* ululō, ululāre (Rv. 14)
(to) **hurry,** *verb,* properō, properāre (Rv. 12)
in, on, *prep.,* in (+abl) (3)
infant, *noun,* īnfāns, īnfāntis, *m.* (Rv. 24)
insect, *noun,* bestiola, -ae, *f.* (19)
into, *prep.,* in (+acc) (3)
(to) **invite,** *verb,* invītō, invītāre (3)
is, *verb,* est (Rv. 3)

J

jewel, *noun,* gemma, -ae, *f.* (11)
judge, juror, *noun,* iūdex, iūdicis, *m.* (17)
juice, *noun,* sūcus, -ī, *m.* (22)

K

(to) **kick,** *verb,* calcitrō, calcitrāre (12)
king, *noun,* rēx, rēgis, *m.* (Rv. 21)
knight, *noun,* eques, equitis, *m.* (21)

L

lamb, *noun,* agnus, -i, *m.* (5)
land, *noun,* terra, -ae, *f.* (Rv. 12)
large, *adj.,* magnus, -a, -um (10)
(to) **laugh, smile,** *verb,* rīdeō, rīdēre (24)
laurel wreath, *noun,* laurea, -ae, *f.* (13)
law, *noun,* lex, legis, *f.* (16)
(to) **lead,** *verb,* dūco (p. 74)
leaf, *noun,* folium, -ī, *n.* (Rv. 19)
leg, *noun,* crūs, crūris, *n.* (19)
letter, *noun,* littera, -ae, *f.* (1)
(to) **lie down,** *verb,* cubō, cubāre (9)
(to) **lift up,** *verb,* levō, levāre (20)
lion, *noun,* leo, leōnis, *m.* (24)
(to) **listen to,** *verb,* auscultō, auscultāre (Rv. 21)
little, small, *adj.,* parvus, -a, -um (10)
lizard, *noun,* lacerta, -ae, *f.* (19)
log, *noun,* lignum, -ī, *n.* (15)
long, *adj.,* longus, -a, -um (11)
(for a) **long time,** *adv.,* diū (15)
(to) **look at,** *verb,* spectō, spectāre (2)

lord, master, *noun,* dominus, -ī, *m.* (Rv. 4)
lunch, *noun,* prandium, -ī, *n.* (22)

M

maidservant, *noun,* ancilla, -ae, *f.* (3)
(to) **make, create,** *verb,* creō, creāre (18)
male friend, *noun,* amīcus, -ī, *m.,* (2)
male pig, *noun,* porcus, -ī, *m.,* (5)
male teacher, *noun,* magister, magistrī, *m.* (1)
man, *noun,* vir, -ī, *m.* (Rv. 24)
man, old, *noun,* senex, senis, *m.* (Rv. 18)
map, board,, *noun,* tabula, -ae, *f.* (2)
mask, *noun,* persōna, -ae, *f.* (24)
master, lord, *noun,* dominus, -ī, *m.* (Rv. 4)
meadow, *noun,* prātum, -i, *n.* (4)
medicine, *noun,* medicāmentum, -ī, *n.* (9)
(to) **milk,** *verb,* mulgeō, mulgēre (5)
money, *noun,* pecunia, -ae, *f.* (Rv. 12)
monument, *noun,* monumentum, -ī (7)
mossy, *adj.,* muscōsus, -a, -um (15)
mother, *noun,* māter, mātris, *f.* (3)
(to) **move,** *verb,* moveo, -ere (Rv. 12)
mud, *noun,* lutum, -ī, *n.* (22)
music, *noun,* mūsica, -ae, *f.* (21)

N

napkin, *noun,* mappa, -ae, *f.* (8)
nephew, *phrase,* filius sorōris (18)
niece, *phrase,* filia sorōris (18)
night, *noun,* nox, noctis, *f.* (16)
nine, *adj.,* novem (Rv. 8)
ninth, *adj.,* nōnus, -a, -um (13)
not, *adv.,* nōn (Rv. 4)
note well, *phrase,* notā bene (Rv. 1)
now, *adv.,* nunc (15)
number, *noun,* numerus, -ī, *m.* (2)

O

(to) **obey,** *verb,* pareō parēre (16)
ocean, *noun,* ōceanus, -ī, *m.* (23)

Glossary: English to Latin

officer, *noun,* praefectus, -ī, *m.* (17)
often, *adv.,* saepe (15)
old man, *noun,* senex, senis, *m.* (Rv. 18)
olive green, *adj.,* herbacea, -a, -um (p125)
olive oil, *noun,* oleum, -ī, *n.* (6)
olive, olive tree, *noun,* olīva, -ae, *f.* (6)
one, *adj.,* unus, -a, -um (Rv. 8)
opinion, *noun,* sententia, -ae, *f.* (17)
orchard, *noun,* pomarium, -ī, *n.* (Rv. 6)
(to) order, *verb,* imperō, imperāre (17)
over, across, *prep.,* trans(+acc) (23)
to overflow, *verb,* redundō, redundāre (15)

P

parade, *noun,* pompa, -ae, *f.* (21)
parasol, *noun,* umbella, -ae, *f.* (23)
parent, *noun,* parens, parentis, *m. or f.* (16)
parrot, *noun,* psittacus, -ī , *m.* (16)
party, *noun,* convīvium, -ī, *n.* (8)
pear, *noun,* pirum, -ī, *n.* (22)
pearl, *noun,* margarīta, -ae, *f.* (11)
pencil, *noun,* stylus, -ī, *m.* (Rv. 2)
piece, *noun,* frustum, -ī, *n.* (9)
piece of paper, *noun,* charta, -ae, *f.* (Rv. 2)
pig, female, *noun,* porca, -ae, *f.* (5)
pig, little, *noun,* porcellus, - i, *m.* (5)
pig, male, *noun,* porcus, -ī, *m.* (5)
(to) pile up, *verb,* struō, struāre (4)
pill, *noun,* pilula, -ae, *f.* (9)
pink, *adj.,* roseus, -a, -um (10)
plant, *noun,* herba, -ae, *f.* (Rv. 6)
(a) play, *phrase,* lūdus scaenicus, *m.* (24)
(to) plow, *verb,* arō, arāre (5)
(to) point, show , *verb,* monstrō, monstrāre (2)
(to) polish, *verb,* līmo, līmāre (11)
pony, *noun,* mannulus,-i, *m.* (4)

(to) prepare, *verb,* parō, parāre (3)
(to) pretend, copy, *verb,* simulō, simulāre (21)
princess, *phrase,* filia regis, *f.* (21)
prison, *noun,* carcer, carceris, *m.* (17)
(to) prune, *verb,* putō, putāre (6)
public square, *noun,* forum,-i, *n.* (7)
purple, *noun,* purpureus,- a, -um (18)

R

race, *noun,* curriculum, -ī, *n.* (24)
race course, *noun,* circus,- i, *m.* (24)
rain, *noun,* plūvia, -ae, *f.* (22)
(to) recite, *verb,* recitō, recitāre (1)
red, *adj.,* ruber, rubra, rubrum, (10)
reptile, *phrase,* bestia serpens, *f.* (19)
reward, prize, *noun,* praemium, -ī, *n.* (13)
(to) ride on horseback, *verb,* equitō, equitāre (Rv. 4)
ring, *noun,* anulus, -ī, *m.* (11)
river, *noun,* fluvius, -ī, *m.* (15)
riverbank, *noun,* rīpa, -ae, *f.* (15)
road, street, *noun,* via, -ae, *f.* (7)
(to) rob, *verb,* exspoliō, exspoliāre (16)
robber, *noun,* praedo, praedōnis, *m.* (16)
robe of state, *noun,* trabea, -ae, *f.* (21)
rock, *noun,* saxum, -ī, *n.* (4)
rock quarry, *noun,* lapicīdīnae, -arum, *f.* (20)
rock, little , *noun,* saxulum, -ī, *n.* (20)
Rome , *noun,* Rōma,-ae, *f.* (7)
rooster, *noun,* gallus, -i, *m.* (4)
rough, uneven, *adj.,* asper, aspera, asperum (20)
round, *adj.,* rotundus, -a, -um, (12)
ruby, *noun,* carbunculus, -ī, *m.* (20)

S

sand, beach, *noun,* harena, -ae, *f.* (23)
(to) save, *verb,* servō, servāre (15)
(to) say, tell, *verb,* narrō, narrāre (Rv. 9)

scepter, *noun*, sceptrum,-i, *n.* (21)
school, game, *noun*, lūdus, -ī, *m.* (2)
seagull, *noun*, gāvia, -ae, *f.* (23)
seahorse, *noun*, hippocampus, -ī, *m.* (23)
seashore, *phrase*, ōra marītima, *f.* (23)
seat, chair, *noun*, sella, -ae, *f.* (2)
seaweed, *noun*, alga, -ae, *f.* (23)
second, *adj.*, secundus, -a, -um (13)
(to) see, *verb*, videō, vidēre (Rv. 22)
(to) sell, *verb*, venditō, venditāre (11)
senate building, *noun*, cūria, -ae, *f.* (18)
senator, *noun*, senātor, senātōris, *m.* (18)
(to) send away, *verb*, relegō, relegāre (17)
seven, *adj.*, septem (Rv. 8)
seventh, *adj.*, septimus, -a, um (13)
shadow, shade, *noun*, umbra, -ae, *f.* (23)
(to) share, *verb*, commūnicō, commūnicāre (22)
sharp, *adj.*, acūtus, -a, -um (11)
(to) shear, shave, clip, *verb*, tondeō, tondēre (5)
sheep, *noun*, ovis, ovis, *f.* (5)
shepherd, *noun*, pastor, pastōris, *m.* (Rv. 5)
shield, *noun*, scūtum, -ī, *n.* (11)
(to) shine, be bright, *verb*, lūceō, lūcēre (22)
shoe, *noun*, calceus, -ī, *m.* (10)
shop, *noun*, taberna, -ae, *f.* (Rv. 11)
shopkeeper, *noun*, tabernārius, -ī , *m.* (11)
(to) shout, *verb*, clāmō, clamāre (12)
shovel, *noun*, pala, -ae, *f.* (Rv. 6)
(to) show, point out, *verb*, monstrō, monstrāre (2)
sick, *adj.*, aeger, aegra, aegrum (8)
(to be) sick, *verb*, aegrōtō, aegrōtāre (9)
sickness, *noun*, morbus, -ī, *m.* (9)
silver, money, *adj.*, argentum, -ī, *n.* (13)

(to) sing, *verb*, cantō, cantāre (Rv. 8)
sister, *noun*, soror, sorōris, *f.* (3)
(to) sit, *verb*, sedeō, sedēre (Rv. 15)
six, *adj.*, sex (Rv. 8)
sixth, *adj.*, sextus, -a, -um (13)
slave, servant, *noun*, servus, -ī, *m.* (3)
(to) slip, stumble, *verb*, lapsō, lapsāre (20)
slow, *adj.*, tardus, -a, -um (12)
small, little, *adj.*, parvus, -a, -um (10)
smoke, *noun*, fūmus, -ī, *m.* (8)
snake, *noun*, serpens, serpentis *m.* or *f.* (19)
soldier, *noun*, mīles, mīlitis, *m.* (17)
song, *noun*, carmen, carminis, *n.* (21)
(to) sound, *verb*, sonō, sonāre (22)
speaker, *noun*, ōrātor, ōrātōris, *m.*(21)
speech, *noun*, ōrātio, ōrātiōnis, *f.* (21)
spider, *noun*, arānea, -ae, *f.* (19)
(to) spin, weave, *verb*, neō, nēre (19)
stage, *noun*, scaena, -ae, *f.* (24)
stall, stable, *noun*, stabulum, -ī, *n.* (Rv. 4)
(to) stand, *verb*, stō, stāre (7)
(to) stand near, *verb*, astō, astāre (14)
statue, *noun*, statua,-ae, *f.* (7)
stealthily, *adv.*, furtim (16)
stick out, *verb (imp.)*, ostendē (9)
stomach, *noun*, stomachus, -ī, *m.* (8)
stomach ache, *phrase*, dolor stomachī (9)
stone, rock, *noun*, lapis, lapidis, *m.* (20)
stony, *adj.*, lapidōsus, -a, -um (20)
story, *noun*, fābula, -ae, *f.* (2)
street, road,, *noun*, via,-ae, *f.* (7)
(to) strengthen, *verb*, firmō, firmāre (15)
(to) study, *verb*, studeō, studēre (2)
student, boy, *noun.*, discipulus, -ī, *m.* (1)

student, girl, *noun.,* discipula, -ae, *f.* (1)
suddenly, *adv.,* repente (15)
sun, *noun,* sōl, sōlis, *m.* (22)
(to) swallow, *verb,* dēvorō, dēvorāre (9)
(to) swim, *verb,* nō, nāre (15)
sword, *noun,* gladius, -ī, *m.* (21)

T

tall, high, *adj.,* altus, -a, -um (12)
(to) taste, *verb,* lībō, lībāre (Rv. 4)
teacher, female, *noun,* magistra, -ae, *f.* (1)
teacher, male, *noun,* magister, magistrī, *m.* (1)
(to) tell, say, *verb,* narrō, narrāre (Rv. 9)
temple, *noun,* templum, -ī, *n.* (7)
ten, *adj.,* decem (Rv. 8)
tenth, *adj.,* decimus, -a, -um (13)
testimony, *noun,* testimōnium, -ī, *n.* (17)
theater, *noun,* theātrum, -ī, *n.* (24)
then, *adv.,* tum (15)
third, *adj.,* tertius, -a, -um (13)
three, *adj.,* tres (Rv. 8)
through, *prep.,* per (+acc) (12)
(to) throw, *verb,* iactō, iactāre (12)
(to) throw stones at, *verb,* lapidō, lapidāre (20)
thunder, *noun,* tonitrus, -us, *m.* (22)
(to) tickle, *verb,* tītillō, tītillāre (19)
tiger, *noun,* tigris, tigris, *m.* (24)
to, toward, *prep.,* ad (+acc) (3)
today, *adv.,* hodiē (14)
toga, *noun,* toga, -ae, *f.* (10)
tomorrow, *adv.,* crās (14)
tongue, *noun,* lingua, -ae, *f.* (9)
treasure, *noun,* thēsaurus, -ī, *m.* (14)
tree, *noun,* arbor, arboris, *f.* (Rv. 19)
tree cricket, *noun,* cicāda, -ae, *f.* (19)
trial, court, *noun,* iūdicium, -ī, *n.* (17)
tunic, *noun,* tunica, -ae, *f.* (Rv. 10)
two, *adj.,* duo (Rv. 8)

U

ugly, *adj.,* foedus, -a, -um (11)
uncle, *noun,* avūnculus, -ī, *m.* (18)
uneven, rough, *adj.,* asper, aspera, asperum (20)

V

vineyard, *noun,* vinea, -ae, *f.* (Rv. 6)
(to) visit, *verb,* visitō, visitāre (3)

W

(to) wait for, *verb,* exspectō, exspectare (14)
(to) walk, *verb,* ambulō, ambulāre (3)
wall, *noun,* mūrus, -ī, *m.* (12)
(to) wander, err, *verb,* errō, errāre (7)
(to) warn, *verb,* moneō, monēre (9)
water, *noun,* aqua, -ae, *f.* (5)
wave, *noun,* unda, -ae, *f.* (23)
(to) wear, *verb,* gestō, gestāre (24)
(to) weave, spin, *verb,* neō, nēre (19)
web, *noun,* tela, -ae, *f.* (19)
well, *adv.,* bene (15)
What is it?, *phrase,* Quid est? (Rv. 1)
(to) whistle, hiss (at), *verb,* sībilō, sībilāre (16)
white, *adj.,* albus, -a, -um (10)
Who is it?, *phrase,* Quis est? (Rv. 1)
wide, *adj.,* lātus, -a, -um (12)
wild animal, *noun,* ferus, -ī, *m.* (14)
wind, *noun,* ventus, -ī, *m.* (22)
window, *noun,* fenestra, -ae, *f.* (12)
wine, *noun,* vinum, -ī, *n.* (Rv. 6)
with, *prep.,* cum (+abl) (6)
witness, *noun,* testis, testis, *m. or f.* (17)
wool, *noun,* lāna, -ae, *f.* (5)
(to) work, *verb,* labōrō, labōrāre (5)

Y

year, *noun,* annus, -ī, *m.* (8)
yellow, blond, *adj.,* flāvus, -a, -um (10)
yesterday, *adv.,* herī (14)

Index

Ablative case, 45, 80

Accusative case, 35, 42

Accusative plural, 36

Accusative singular, 36,

Ad (preposition with acc.) 42,

Adjectives, 123, 127, 131, 165

Adverbs, 57, 165

Amō Chant (see First Conjugation Chant)

Audiō Chant (see Fourth Conjugation Chant)

Base of a noun (see noun base)

Cardinal numbers, 100, 155,

Case endings, 25,

Case, adjectives, 131,

Commands , 69, 75,

Compound subject nouns, 33,

Conjugate, LL1

Dative case, 103

Declension, 25, 91

Demonstrative Pronoun Singular Chant, LL1

Demonstrative Pronoun Plural Chant, LL1

Derivative, 19

Direct object, 35, 36

Dūcō Chant (see third conjugation), 74

Feminine, 123, 156, 165

Fifth Declension Chant, 154, 178

First Conjugation Chant, LL1

First conjugation verbs, 22, 65,

First Declension Chant, LL1, 20, 25, 45, 185, 203

First declension noun endings ("A" Family), 25

Four principal parts, 60

Fourth Conjugation Chant, 90, 116

Fourth Declension Chant, 130, 149

Fourth Declension Neuter Chant, 138, 149

Future Tense Verb Ending Chant, 30, 32, 194

Future Passive Verb Ending Chant, LL1

Future Tense Verb Endings Chant, LL1

Gender, adjectives, 123

Genitive case, 91, 92, 93

Imperative (see Command)

Imperfect Active Verb Ending Chant, LL1

Imperfect Passive Verb Ending Chant, LL1

Imperfect Tense Verb Ending Chant, LL1, 40, 41, 194, 65

"In a Nutshell", 79

Indirect objects, 102

Infinitive, 53, 60, 61, 65

Interrogative, 76, 77, 79

Linking verb, 54, 59, 257, 276

Linking Verb (Future Tense), 265

Linking Verb (Imperfect Tense), 275

Linking Verb (Future Tense) Chant, 265

Linking Verb (Imperfect Tense) Chant, 275, 276

Linking Verb (Present Tense) Chant, LL1, 54, 59, 256

Macaronic story, 176, 284

Masculine, 123, 124, 156

Neuter, 123, 124, 156, 226

Nominative case, 25, , 258, 276

Nominative plural, 26
Nominative singular, 26, 122
Non (adverb), 57
Notā bene, 20, 26,
Noun base, 92
Noun cases, five, 26
Noun endings (see case endings)
Number, adjectives, 127
Object of the preposition, 42
Ordinal numbers, 156
Pattern 1 sentence, 17, 26,
Pattern 2 sentence, 17, 35, 55
Pattern 3 sentences, 17, 104, 231
Pattern 4 sentence, 17, 258
Perfect Tense Verb Endings Chant, LL1
Personal Pronoun First Person Chant, LL1
Personal Pronoun Second Person Chant, LL1
Pluperfect Tense Verb Endings Chant, LL1
Plural command, 70
Possessive nouns, 93
Possessive Noun Adjective , 96,
Possum Chant , 54, 59, 84, 139
Predicate noun, 258, 276
Preposition, 42, 45, 80
Present Passive Verb Ending Chant, LL1
Present tense verb endings, 21, 65
Present Tense Verb Ending Chant, LL1, 20, 21, 194
Questions (see interrogative)
Second Conjugation Chant , LL1
Second conjugation verbs, 31, 66
Second Declension Chant, LL1, 20, 25, 45, 185, 203
Second Declension Neuter Chant, LL1, 54-55, 84, 185
Second declension noun endings ("US" Family), 25
Second principal part (see infinitive), 53, 60

Singular command, 69-, 70
Subject noun, 26, 76
Sum Chant (see linking verb, present tense)
Tense, 275, 276
Third Conjugation Chant, 74, 85
Third Declension Chant, 108, 116, 148, 185, 190
Third Declension I-Stem Chant, 122, 148, 190, 240
Third Declension Neuter Chant, 220, 221, 240, 251
Verb endings, 21
Verb stem, 65
Verb transitive, 36
Videō Chant (see Second conjugation)